THE TRACTION LIBRARY

Want even better results and more business success?

Every person on your team must be equipped with the right information and tools to implement EOS®, the Entrepreneurial Operating System® purely throughout your organization. With The Traction Library, your entire company—from leadership to management to employees—will understand their role and be better equipped to help your company succeed.

──────── HERE'S HOW! ────────

AVAILABLE BOOKS	WHO IT'S FOR
Traction	For everyone
Rocket Fuel	For the Visionary and the Integrator
Get a Grip (Traction's Fable)	For the leadership team
How to Be a Great Boss	For leaders, managers, and supervisors
What the Heck Is EOS?	For all employees, managers, and supervisors
The EOS Life	For everyone

Visit **www.eosworldwide.com** to get everything you need to fully implement EOS® in your company today.

THE

E◯S

LIFE

ALSO BY GINO WICKMAN

Traction
Get a Grip (with Mike Paton)
Rocket Fuel (with Mark C. Winters)
How to Be a Great Boss (with Rene Boer)
What the Heck Is EOS? (with Tom Bouwer)
Entrepreneurial Leap

THE EOS LIFE

How to Live Your Ideal Entrepreneurial Life

GINO WICKMAN

BenBella Books, Inc.
Dallas, TX

 BenBella Books, Inc.
10440 N. Central Expressway
Suite 800
Dallas, TX 75231
benbellabooks.com
Send feedback to feedback@benbellabooks.com

BenBella is a federally registered trademark.

Printed in the United States of America
10 9 8 7 6 5 4 3 2

Library of Congress Control Number: 2021012419
ISBN 9781637740132
eISBN 9781637740149

Copyediting by James Fraleigh
Proofreading by Michael Fedison and Cape Cod Compositors, Inc.
Text design and composition by Aaron Edmiston
Interior illustrations by Drew Robinson Spork Design
Cover design by Sarah Avinger
Lightbulb artwork by Media Bridge Advertising

Special discounts for bulk sales are available.
Please contact bulkorders@benbellabooks.com.

To all of the EOS Implementers in the world, thank you for the work that you do and your commitment to the cause.

You are making a huge impact on entrepreneurs, businesses, people, and their families. The real-world stories you contributed to this book brought it to life.

You are truly putting a dent in the universe.

CONTENTS

If you are a reader who is not familiar with the Entre-preneurial Operating System (EOS), *Traction*, or the EOS tools, that's okay. I've written this book in such a way that it will make sense. However, if you want to increase your understanding of EOS and the tools, please read *Traction: Get a Grip on Your Business*. You can also download all of the tools mentioned in this book at eoslife.com.

FOREWORD

I first met Gino in September 2005 after 27 years of being an entrepreneur and an owner of two businesses. I worked long hours seven days a week and had many dreams, some realized, some not. Gino introduced me to a set of simple tools, systematically taught and implemented, to help entrepreneurs clarify and get what they want most from their businesses. I couldn't help but imagine how different my life and business experiences would have been had I started my journey with his tools. Those thoughts compelled me to partner with Gino to take EOS, the Entrepreneurial Operating System, to the world. We set a goal of helping 10,000 entrepreneurial leadership teams run on EOS.

After seven years as Gino's partner, I started to notice an important complementary benefit to his work practices. EOS wasn't just a business system. It was how Gino lived every day of his life—applying proven life principles through simple, practical tools to create a better, richer life. As we built EOS Worldwide and brought it to a global audience, I found that my life, too, was better and richer. While working with my own client leadership teams, I started to observe the same benefits showing up in their lives as they reported their personal and professional good news in sessions. I also started to notice our expanding community of EOS Implementers expressing the same personal satisfaction.

What was going on? I had to find words to articulate what was happening. Suddenly, I realized that all of us were doing what we loved, with people we loved, making a huge difference in the world, being compensated appropriately for the value we were delivering, and having the time to pursue other passions. That was it!

This book provides context for all of the other books in the Traction Library. All of those instructional books provide the means to this end—or, for many of us, a new beginning. Yet *The EOS Life* brings it all together by focusing on how EOS changes not just our businesses but our lives. It reveals the behind-the-scenes story and gives you insights into achieving this lifestyle for yourself. Gino has done a great job articulating benefits that we didn't see or understand in the beginning, and I'm confident that by the time you turn the last page, you'll be eager to start living The EOS Life.

This isn't hype or a pipe dream. This book is a guide to real, deep satisfaction. I invite you to join me in living The EOS Life.

**—Don Tinney, cofounder of EOS Worldwide
and the second EOS Implementer**

THE EOS LIFE

You deserve to live your ideal life.

Sadly, most entrepreneurs and leaders don't. This book was written to change that.

Imagine doing what you love to do every day. What gives you unlimited energy? So much so that you wake up before your alarm clock every morning. Picture doing it with energy and excitement, and with people you really love being around. People who are enjoyable and uplifting. Picture the work you are doing making an impact. The impact *you* want to make, whether it's on the world, your country, state, or community. On your employees, clients/customers, family, friends, or yourself. Also imagine you are being compensated well, making as much money as you want, while also having the time to pursue the other activities you are passionate about in your personal life. That might be hiking, golfing, painting, playing an instrument, reading, bird watching, or traveling. You might like helping your church, doing charitable work, or spending time with friends and family.

This is 100% possible, and I'm about to show you how.

THE QUESTION THAT LAUNCHED THE EOS LIFE

I haven't spent my entire business career living what is now known as The EOS Life. The truth is, I let the busy part of business overtake me so much that I was nowhere near living my ideal life . . . until a brief, piercing conversation added the final piece to the puzzle.

Throughout my twenties I was fortunate enough to have incredible experiences guided by special mentors. I was a sponge for knowledge. I couldn't get enough. I sacrificed almost everything else to learn, grow, and become successful.

Running my dad's business, turning it around, then selling it kept me on my toes and taught me a lot. My dad taught me his years of entrepreneurial experience. My mentor Sam Cupp masterfully showed me how to run a successful business. These lessons pounded through my head day and night. What Oliver Wendell Holmes Sr. once said is true: "A mind, once expanded by a new idea, never returns to its former dimensions."

I joined Entrepreneurs' Organization (EO), surrounded myself with fellow entrepreneurs, and absorbed their knowledge, ambitions, and elements of mastery. I was coached by one of my greatest mentors, Dan Sullivan, through whom I discovered my Unique Ability® and the Entrepreneurial Time System®. I studied the teachings of Jim Rohn, Earl

Nightingale, Les Brown, Michael Gerber, Napoleon Hill, Tony Robbins, Stephen Covey, and Brian Tracy. I devoured dozens of books and audio recordings. I also attended countless conferences, seminars, and events.

Literally hundreds of lessons have shaped my thinking and belief system.

From these great teachers and experiences, I developed a philosophy that's a part of my daily Modus Operandi (M.O.): how to function, think, live, breathe, and talk. How to create freedom, maximize my time, and increase my productivity. I learned the risk/reward equation. How to serve people and add value. Equally as important, I learned that it's okay to do what you love and make a lot of money.

This work system made me a great worker, but it left out one vital ingredient: life balance.

Then, in my late twenties, just as I was putting the finishing touches on my operating system, I had a wake-up call—a simple question shifted the way I spend my time.

Early one morning, when my daughter was four years old, I was getting into my car to head off to work. Before I could close the door, she came out of the house and up to the car. I looked down with a big smile and said, "Hi, sweetie."

Then came the question that changed my life. She asked, "Daddy, are you going home?"

My jaw dropped. I was crushed. "Going home?"

I looked at her and said, "No, Alexis, Daddy lives *here*. I'm going to work."

What I'd been overlooking hit me like a ton of bricks. Until then I was rarely home, because I worked morning until night.

I committed, right on the spot, to having a more balanced life. That "aha!" moment combined with everything I had learned, and The EOS Life was born. Only I wouldn't call it that, not yet.

THE HISTORY OF THE EOS LIFE

I had my first glimpse of the personal impact of The EOS Life five years after creating EOS. I was making a decision to rebrand and reposition EOS for marketing purposes. To that end I engaged a high-end marketing firm. They asked for a list of my best clients so they could talk to them and learn what the process was doing for them. Seven hard-charging entrepreneurs were selected from the list, who quickly came to be called "the Magnificent Seven."

Over the next few weeks, the marketing firm interviewed each of the Magnificent Seven. They then returned with the feedback. Eager to hear the outcome, I expected to hear things like, "Our company is growing faster than ever," "We are making more profit than ever," "The chaos we used to experience is gone," and "The company is finally running like a Swiss watch." Those were the results they were experiencing.

But the feedback turned out to be quite different.

The owner of the marketing firm started the meeting by saying, "We have the feedback from each of your clients, and it is eerily similar." He continued: "Every client, seven out of seven, unanimously said the same thing. Out of the many benefits, they said the number-one result of implementing EOS in their companies was 'a better quality of life.'"

I was shocked. I didn't know what to make of this remarkable by-product of the system. And I didn't consider what "The EOS Life" really meant until almost seven years after that marketing meeting, when my partner, Don Tinney, made its benefits clear.

He talked about the life he and I were living, the life our clients and EOS Implementers were living. He came to call it The EOS Life. Don memorialized the new term when he presented it at one of the quarterly meetings for all of our EOS Implementers. They liked it instantly.

Yet its broader meaning didn't fully sink in for me. I was still focusing on the business results.

A few years later, I was asked to keynote the first-ever EOS Conference, which has become an annual event for leaders running their company on EOS. I wasn't quite sure what my topic would be, since all of the attendees already knew all of the EOS tools. I was half asleep in a hotel room in Los Angeles when I had a "Eureka!" moment: "The topic has to be The EOS Life." At 4 AM I got up and wrote out the entire speech. The words flowed like water.

The talk at the EOS Conference was a big hit. I delivered the same keynote speech three years in a row at our annual conferences, each time adding more finishing touches. I figured out how to articulate the full parameters of what The EOS Life was, so it could inspire tens of thousands of people to live their ideal life.

That is the purpose of this book. To give you everything you need to live your ideal life.

I never thought I'd write these words. I never intended to write another EOS book after writing the previous five Traction Library books. Out of the blue, though, on a typical day in the middle of the week, a sense of urgency came over me, and I said to myself, "I need to write the EOS Life book." I hope that it has a tremendous impact on your life.

WHAT IS THE EOS LIFE?

Now that you know how The EOS Life evolved, let's shift to exactly what it is.

The EOS Life is you doing what you love, with people you love, while making a huge difference, being compensated appropriately, and having time for other passions.

This life is absolutely achievable and 100% customizable for who you uniquely are.

First you have to believe you are worthy of living this way. As I mentioned at the beginning of this chapter, sadly, most entrepreneurs don't live their ideal life. Maybe that's because you don't feel you deserve it or are afraid of it, you are too undisciplined, you have some deep-seated, self-destructive psychological disorder, or you simply don't know how. This book will solve all of that. As spiritual teacher and author David R. Hawkins wrote, "The unconscious will allow us to have only what we think we deserve." I'll do everything in my power to convince you that you deserve it, and show you how to get it, but you have to believe you are worthy in order for it to become a reality. And the beauty is, many people will benefit from your achieving this life.

This book will not tell you what you should love to do or who you should do it with. It won't say how much money you should make, what impact you should have on the world, or what your other passions should be. You are in charge of deciding all of that. Instead, this book will create the context that gives you the clarity to make those decisions.

WHO THIS BOOK IS FOR

EOS was created to help entrepreneurs. It helps them get everything they want from their business.

So, first and foremost, this book is for entrepreneurs. Yet the opportunity to live The EOS Life will spread far beyond that. This book is for leadership team members, too. It can also have a huge impact on the rest of a company's employees, as well as their families and loved ones.

Another audience for this book is the EOS Implementers around the world. These are successful entrepreneurs who help companies implement EOS. (Some companies self-implement EOS and some use an EOS Implementer to assist them.)

Most of the stories you'll read will be about entrepreneurs, who I'll call "Visionaries" for the rest of this book. But I'll also share examples of the incredible impact of The EOS Life on leadership team members and EOS Implementers. Every one of the stories features real EOS clients, because they were submitted by EOS Implementers.

If you have started implementing EOS in your company, you are already on the path to enjoying these benefits. Just like the Magnificent Seven that shared why they love EOS, tens of thousands of companies are now sharing in the benefits of The EOS Life. Now you need to understand the tools on a much deeper level, so that you can live your ideal life to the fullest.

EOS has specific tools, disciplines, and philosophies that will guide you toward The EOS Life. This book breaks out those individual tools in different chapters, so that you can clearly understand how to use them. By helping you grasp how these business tools affect you personally, it will help you move the needle faster toward living your ideal life.

I subscribe to Buckminster Fuller's belief: "If you want to teach people a new way of thinking, don't bother trying to teach them. Instead, give them a tool, the use of which will lead to new ways of thinking."

LET THE JOURNEY BEGIN

First, you must understand the five major points of The EOS Life:

1. Doing what you love
2. With people you love
3. Making a huge difference
4. Being compensated appropriately
5. With time for other passions

We'll dive into each of those points, chapter by chapter. Each chapter will have questions to answer and actions to take. Please use a journal while reading this book, or write in the blank pages provided at the end of each chapter. You can also purchase The EOS Life Journal/Planner at eoslife .com, which was created to be the perfect complement to this book. When you write down what you're learning, you'll better anchor those points in your mind. Also, countless studies have shown how much more effective it is to write by hand than type. You retain more, you spark your creativity, and you learn more. Once you finish this book, I urge you to review your journal/notes every quarter going forward.

Let's begin your journey by drawing the following EOS Life Model in your journal:

Drawing the above model in your journal will start bringing The EOS Life into fruition for yourself. If you haven't figured it out yet, that's you in the center. Think about how you can live what's in those five circles every single day.

Once you have finished reading the book, we'll return to this model to gauge where you are on your journey.

At the end of this book, I added a special bonus "minibook" that will teach you a way to harness, manage, and expand your energy. The mini-book contains 10 disciplines that are the perfect complement to The EOS Life. I've been living by The 10 Disciplines for more than 20 years with great success. You might find them to be a pleasant surprise and highly valuable, as many have.

Let's move to the next step in your journey by diving into the first point of living The EOS Life: doing what you love.

Chapter 1

DOING WHAT YOU LOVE

"Where your talents and the needs of the world
cross, lies your calling, vocation, purpose."
—Aristotle

You have a genetic encoding that is unique to you. You have a talent or superpower. You have a personal sweet spot. There is something that you love to do and that you are great at doing. You are passionate about it. It is your purpose.

Your job is to figure out exactly what that is. And once you are clear on it, you should spend all of your working time doing it.

What kind of work do you love to do?

> **Take Five:** Please take a few minutes right now and ponder this question. Write down in your journal everything that comes to mind. Do you like solving problems, working with clients, leading people, creating products or services?
>
> Then rate yourself on a scale of 1–10. How close are you to doing what you love 100% of your working time? Ten is the highest. That's the ultimate goal.

You must avoid trying to be all things to all people, trying to do it all, trying to be good at everything. All greatness comes from focusing. If you are like most people, you're trying to do everything. You're trying to be everything. Well, you're never going to be great if that is the case. Figure out that one thing that you were put here to do, focus on it, and you will be happy, fulfilled, and energized.

To paraphrase a popular saying, the two most important days in your life are the day you are born and the day you find out why.

This soul-searching could possibly lead you to realize that you're in the wrong business. That was the case with Todd Sachse of Sachse Construction Company, who started out with a maid service company and a window-washing business. After a few years he realized he didn't love the business of "cleaning toilets," as he describes it. He sold those businesses once he realized his passion for the construction industry. He has since built a $200 million general contracting company and does what he loves every day.

Sometimes the soul-searching leads to a career change, like a lawyer in Chicago who became an attorney because that's what his family wanted him to do. He hated it. He later found his love for real estate sales, and he's now one of the top realtors in Illinois.

Sometimes you merely need to tweak your job description, like the Visionary business owner who delegated all of her finance-department responsibilities to free herself up to do what she loved.

Regardless of what you discover, it's vital you discover it.

In each chapter, after I explain the corresponding point, I then share the EOS tool or tools that will help you live that particular point in The EOS Life. Let's begin with the first one.

THE EOS TOOL THAT
MAKES THIS HAPPEN

The tool that helps you discover what you love to do is called Delegate and Elevate. You may know the tool already, but if not, here's a refresher, because it's the ultimate tool for helping you to determine your personal sweet spot.

Start by listing everything you do at work. Typically, you'll draw up a laundry list of at least 20 things. Take a few minutes right now. Write "Laundry List" at the top of your journal page and list everything, like checking email, meetings, solving employee issues, paperwork, talking to customers, and so forth. List everything work related that you do all day, every day.

Next, copy the following tool in your journal. Take up the entire page so you have room to write.

Now, put each of your laundry list items into one of the four quadrants. Let's start with the worst of the bunch. In the bottom right-hand quadrant, write everything that you don't like to do and you're not good at doing. We all do some of those things.

Next, in the bottom left-hand quadrant, write all the things you don't like to do, but you're good at. This is most people's personal hell. They have a job that they're good at but don't like doing, and they don't know how to get out. This purgatory for you may include jobs like handling customer service problems, managing people, running meetings, doing paperwork, or managing inventory.

Now let's get to the good stuff. In the top right-hand quadrant, place all the things that you like to do and you're good at. Not such a bad place to be. You don't necessarily spring out of bed to do these tasks, but you don't mind doing them. They are enjoyable to you.

DELEGATE AND ELEVATE™

Love Doing It and Great at Doing It	Like Doing It and Good at Doing It
Don't Like Doing It and Good at Doing It	Don't Like Doing It and Not Good at Doing It

Left for last are the things you love to do and are great at doing—your genetic encoding. Put them in the top left-hand quadrant. Typically, you'll only list two, three, four, maybe five things. Not a lot.

The typical Visionary loves jobs like research and development of products and services, building relationships, creative problem solving, selling, spending time with customers or clients, focusing on growth, building culture, strategic planning, and coming up with ideas.

As a result of this exercise, you will realize that you are doing a lot of things you should not be doing. For a typical Visionary, these might include managing people, running day-to-day operations, holding people accountable, following through with projects, following up on details, paperwork, checking emails, or anything administrative. Your job is to "delegate" everything in the bottom quadrants and "elevate" yourself to the jobs in the top quadrants.

Yet you won't always delegate things. Sometimes you merely need to stop doing them altogether. Are they really necessary? What if no one did them? If they don't benefit the company very much, just stop doing them.

For some, this process of delegating and elevating is freeing. For others, it causes guilt or the feeling that you lack the worthiness to free yourself.

Whatever emotions it prompts for you, identifying your tasks is a great first step toward personal freedom, happiness, and higher productivity and impact.

Yet this is only the beginning. The process of moving toward doing what you love to do all day, every day, is a journey. You're not going to finish this exercise today and enjoy The EOS Life tomorrow, but you're going to be one step closer.

Trixie Whyte is the passionate Visionary of Q2 HR Solutions Group of Companies, one of the largest HR services companies in the Philippines. Before EOS, Trixie was buried in the weeds of her company, constantly pulled in all directions.

After running her business on EOS for a year, she built a structure that allowed her to create an opening for a strong Integrator, Sarah McLeod. (Integrators are the people who run the day-to-day business: presidents, COOs, general managers, etc.) With Sarah in her new role, Trixie was able to delegate and elevate. She gave Sarah control over all of the details involved in running daily operations. This freed up Trixie to spend all of her time on big ideas and relationships, building the company culture, uplifting lives, and growing the business. She is doing what she loves.

Or, let's look at an Integrator, Robby Hagelstein. He is a second-generation leader of URS Medical, which takes care of individuals who need longer-term medical supplies and equipment, as well as mothers who need breast pumps. Robby had taken over running the family business after his dad had moved up to the Visionary role. At first, he thought he had to "do it all," not only to prove to his dad that he could run the company, but also to prove to the employees that he was worthy of filling his dad's shoes. Yet, once he implemented EOS, he realized that he was holding the company back and instead needed to focus on his strengths.

Once he filled out the Delegate and Elevate tool, he achieved clarity. He met with his leadership team, which then consisted of his dad and two brothers-in-law, and discussed what must come off his plate. The two biggies were handling the company finances and dealing with medical insurance companies. They had a young man in the company with the potential to do the delegated jobs, and they offered him the responsibilities. He took the job and knocked it out of the park, quickly earning his way onto the leadership team. Robby was freed up to do what he was good at—running a business and executing strategy. The company is doing better than ever, and Robby continues to delegate other things as the company grows.

Remember, you're trying to move the needle. Make progress toward being in your sweet spot. Some people have a lightbulb moment and make massive changes quickly, and others make steady progress over time. Either track is okay, as long as you are moving in the right direction.

It is amazing to watch the impact that delegating and elevating has on a person, when they realize what they love to do and then give themselves the freedom to do it. Here are a few more examples.

A CFO realized she did not love her role and responsibilities (finance, IT, HR, office management). She also realized that her head of accounting had the skill set, capacity, and passion to take the role, so they swapped. (This was a shocker for everyone in the company.) Now they are both incredibly productive and love their new jobs.

Or, an incredible salesperson was promoted to sales manager, only to realize she absolutely hated managing people. As a result, she stepped down, got back to selling full-time, and became the top-producing salesperson.

Or the EOS client who realized that, while he loved his company, becoming an EOS Implementer was his true calling. As a result, he sold his company and began helping many other firms become successful.

I could list thousands of these transformational stories. But let's spend a little extra time on one particular type—a Visionary who finally spends all of their time doing what they love.

They typically don't start out that way. Usually, a wild and crazy entrepreneur starts a company and builds it through brute force and sheer will. As the company expands, they find themselves buried in the day-to-day details, doing things they don't love. They work morning till night. They are burned out, tired, and miserable.

Along comes EOS, which supplies the lightbulb moment that helps them discover what they love to do. They then find their perfect Integrator to run the day-to-day. They build a leadership team to delegate everything that isn't in their personal sweet spot. By shedding those tasks, they free themselves to grow the company to the next level.

I should point out that, at first, such a Visionary often experiences a feeling of being "put out to pasture." Releasing the reins is a blow to their ego and perceived value. They are no longer the superhero who always saves the day. But once those psychological issues subside, the feeling of freedom blossoms. The Visionary rediscovers the reason they started the company. The company then takes off for the next stage of success.

DELEGATE ONE THING PER QUARTER

With your Delegate and Elevate tool filled out, your next job is to delegate everything in the bottom two quadrants and elevate yourself to the top two quadrants. How quickly you do this is up to you. The best way to measure your progress is to review it every quarter. Every 90 days you must delegate at least one item from the bottom two quadrants to ultimately free yourself to concentrate only on the top two quadrants, your true skill set.

I've been delegating one thing per quarter for 30 years. After a while it gets tricky finding things to delegate because you're offloading only good stuff. It got so good for me that to free my energy, I had to delegate the ownership of an entire company. Once I realized that the responsibilities of owning EOS Worldwide had become a distraction from the things I really loved to do (writing books, creating content, helping entrepreneurs), I decided to sell the company.

Once you compile your laundry list of activities—the "stuff" you're doing with all of your working time—you can see more clearly which ones fit in your sweet spot. That's the stuff you were born to do. It's like a block of marble waiting to be sculpted. As the common axiom goes, the sculpture is already complete within the marble block—you just have to chisel away the superfluous material.

It's time for you to chip away all of the unnecessary "marble" so you can fully realize your genetic encoding.

At EOS Worldwide, the process is made deliberate. Every EOS Implementer is taught that, once they have 10 clients, they should hire a part-time assistant. This assistant does everything that is not in the EOS Implementer's top left-hand quadrant. Things like managing email, scheduling, ordering materials, all paperwork, reporting, booking travel, bookkeeping, and session setup and preparation. This frees the EOS Implementer to find additional clients, manage client sessions, communicate with clients, and continue their education so they can master their craft and provide further value to their clients.

Think of it as a journey. Once you delegate everything in the bottom two quadrants, you should delegate everything in the top right. You should be spending all of your time in the top left-hand quadrant. This is your personal sweet spot: the ultimate goal, doing the stuff you love and are great at doing 100% of your working time.

As I mentioned, Dan Sullivan has been one of my greatest mentors. For 23 years I have been a student of the Strategic Coach® program he founded. He has had a profound impact on me as a business owner, entrepreneur, and Visionary, and has helped over 20,000 entrepreneurs. Dan calls this sweet spot your Unique Ability®. He believes that the definition of your life's purpose is "infinitely expanding your unique ability through greater personal freedom." He thinks it is vital that you get rid of what exhausts you and replace it with what energizes you.

Think about the activities that give you energy. Only you can decide this—no one can decide for you. If someone else did, they could have an ulterior motive, or at least a bias. Likewise, when you move toward your Unique Ability, make sure that positive emotions are driving you and not negative emotions. Heed the warning of the great motivational speaker Les Brown: "Too many of us are not living our dream because we are living our fears."

As you begin to delegate and elevate, you may feel guilty because you don't feel it's right to dump that "crappy" stuff you don't like to do on other people. Well, we all love to do different things, and you likely know people who love doing at least some of the stuff you don't like to do. Don't rob others of the chance to do their top-quadrant work just because it's in your lower quadrants. Think of it as a win-win situation.

For some, all of this make sense. But they are unwilling to hire someone to delegate to, either because they are afraid to spend the money, don't think they can afford it, or are too cheap. Well, it is simple math. When you free yourself up to do the things you love, you typically grow faster, earn more money, and become able to afford it. I have found that it is a five-to-one ratio: for every dollar I spend on someone to free me up, I earn $5 in additional productivity, output, or revenue generation.

What also might happen is that you will need to have a tough conversation with someone who is *preventing* you from delegating and elevating. You have to address the people who are forcing, shaming, or manipulating you to stay in the bottom two quadrants. You need to confront them; otherwise you'll never be free.

In some cases, a Visionary may be held back by an Integrator who is resentful that their counterpart gets to have so much fun helping clients, while they are stuck in the day-to-day business. Or a VP of Operations wants to spend more time managing people and working on process improvement to run a better department, but the Visionary owner is a controlling, stubborn micro-manager who refuses to allow one more person to be hired in Operations to free up the VP.

When one person is not letting you fully flourish, you need to discuss this with them. Prepare well, schedule the meeting, and then very directly state the issue and your proposed solution. You must help them see how they are holding back not just you, but also the entire company, from the next level of growth.

This direct discussion usually solves the problem. Your typical obstacle is being bold enough to have the conversation. Colleagues often don't even realize they are holding you back and will respect you for addressing the issue. But don't just vent; bring a plan for them to consider.

THE ACCOUNTABILITY CHART

Delegate and Elevate is the first EOS tool for living your ideal life. The second tool is the Accountability Chart. This tool helps you determine the right structure for your organization, crystallizes roles and responsibilities, and clarifies who reports to who—basically a supercharged organizational chart.

When complete, it looks something like this.

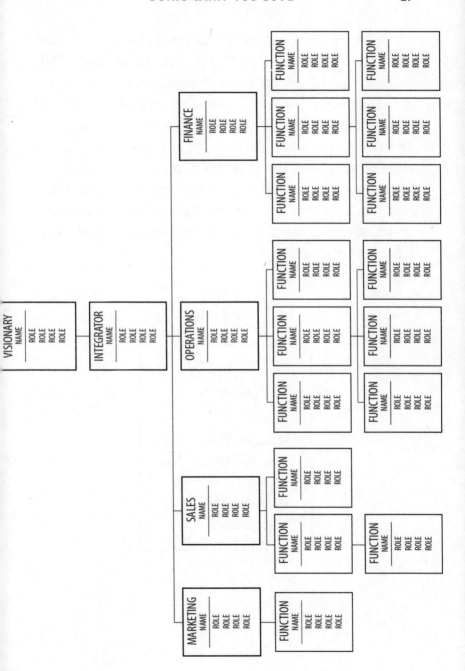

Once your Accountability Chart is complete, each function with its roles is a "seat" that needs to be filled. While there are many benefits of the Accountability Chart in the greater context of EOS (right structure, reporting, roles and responsibilities), the Accountability Chart in the context of The EOS Life has just one goal: the seat you occupy on the chart must reflect your personal sweet spot. If you are the Visionary, make sure your function and your roles reflect that. The same applies if you are the head of marketing, VP of operations, a customer service representative, or whatever function. For example:

```
                    VISIONARY
                    Anna Alvarez
                ─────────────────
                • Culture
                • Company Vision
                • Creative Problem Solving
                • Selling
                • Research and
                  Development
```

If you are the CFO, here's what your seat might look like:

CFO
Liam Wilson

- Lead, Manage, and Accountability
- Finance and Accounting
- Reporting
- IT
- Human Resources

Why will using this tool help you achieve The EOS Life?

By clearly understanding the Delegate and Elevate tool, delegating something every quarter, and ensuring your Accountability Chart seat is a perfect match for you, you will move the needle faster.

Understanding and implementing this first point of The EOS Life—doing what you love—is the main ingredient in the recipe. Each of the following points of The EOS Life will build on each other. As we add the other ingredients, they will expedite the process of your doing what you love and greatly magnify its benefits.

ACTION STEPS

Grab your journal or use the following Notes pages. Please write your answers to these questions:

1. How close are you to doing what you love 100% of your working time?
2. What would it look like to be at 100%?
3. Why aren't you there yet?
4. What would it take to get to 100%?

Write down one thing that you will do in the next seven days to advance you toward doing what you love. You might complete the Delegate and Elevate exercise for the first time. You might pick what to delegate this quarter. You might have a tough conversation with someone holding you back. What will move the needle for you?

NOTES

_____

_____

_____

_____

_____

_____

_____

_____

_____

_____

_____

_____

_____

_____

_____

_____

_____

_____

_____

_____

_____

_____

_____

Chapter 2

WITH PEOPLE YOU LOVE

"You will either look back in life and say
I wish I had, or I'm glad I did."
—Zig Ziglar

'll start this chapter by sharing two extreme ends of a spectrum. On the low end, you can go through life surrounded by people who drain your energy. People you constantly have to push. People who complain about their problems, people who aren't fun to be around. People who make you feel like crap, who make you feel "less than."

Or on the high end, you could surround yourself with people who keep pace with you. People who are uplifting, make you feel good, are energizing, solve problems. People you look forward to being around, who make you better.

In the future, which end of the spectrum would you prefer? Right now, which end of the spectrum are you closer to? As Warren Buffett said, "You move in the direction of the people you associate with."

If the circle you run in is closer to the low end, those people are killing you. Literally. They are draining your energy. You are working harder than you have to. You are carrying too much of the load. You are missing out on the opportunity to enjoy your fullest life. You are not being fair to yourself or them.

Who are the people you love to work with?

Take Five: Please take a few minutes right now and ponder this question. Write down in your journal everyone that comes to mind.

Then rate yourself on a scale of 1–10. How close are you to being surrounded by people you love working with? A 10 means 100% of the people in your work life. That is the ultimate goal.

When your leadership team meets every week, the meeting should be filled with laughter, intense debate, passionate discussion, high trust, and respect. You should look forward to working together and seeing each other.

If you dread meetings and find yourself avoiding your coworkers, there's a problem. That's not living.

Nate Kukla, owner of Unique Indoor Comfort, a four-year-old HVAC company at the time, was starting to see his company plateau. He had seven people on his leadership team and 20 employees. The company had stagnated at $5 million in revenue, not seeing significant growth for the first time. Besides the stalled growth, Nate sensed that the team was not having as much fun as they had the first few years. The leaders were arguing, politicking, and not holding each other and the team accountable.

Once they started the EOS Process, he (and the leadership team) realized that not everyone at the company was in the "right seat." A year later, the leadership team had been invigorated by new members. Just as important, the former members of the leadership team were enjoying success in new roles that were the right seats for them.

The company finished last year with over $15 million in revenue, and Nate turned down a large offer to sell because he's having too much fun with his team.

Regardless of where you are on the spectrum, today is the day to start moving the needle toward the high end.

THE EOS TOOL THAT MAKES THIS HAPPEN

The EOS tool that helps you surround yourself with people you love is the People Analyzer. To fully use the Analyzer, you need to know your company's Core Values. I'll assume you have already discovered those Core Values. If you haven't, please read *Traction: Get a Grip on Your Business* (pp. 35–46) for the Core Value discovery exercise.

You have to be fanatical about knowing your Core Values and surrounding yourself with people that possess them. You start by discovering your Core Values with your leadership team. Then, have your people analyze each other. Each person is given a +, +/-, or a - for how they are living each Core Value. The ones who don't reach the bar (the minimal acceptable level; see the last line of the sample People Analyzer chart) eventually have to go, replaced by people who possess your Core Values. Then you apply the exact same standards with the rest of your employees.

Name	Be Humbly Confident	Grow or Die	Help First	Do the Right Thing	Do What You Say	
THE PEOPLE ANALYZER™						
Charlotte						
Alexander						
Zahra						
Gabriel						
The Bar	+	+	+	+/−	+/−	

You must always hire, fire, review, reward, and recognize with your Core Values in mind. Within one year of doing this, you'll be happier. That's because, on average, 20% of your personnel will have turned over. The ones that didn't fit are gone, replaced by ones who do. Incidentally, the ones that leave typically find a company that aligns with their Core Values and thrive there.

Derek Pittak was the Integrator for TalentLaunch, a Cleveland-based nationwide network of independently operated staffing and recruitment firms under common ownership. Solidifying their Core Values and applying the People Analyzer to everyone opened their eyes. He and his Visionary, Aaron Grossman, removed three members from the leadership team and ultimately removed half of the employees over the next

18 months. The organization is now healthy and continues to grow by finding people with the right cultural alignment.

Similarly, EOS Implementer Gregg Saunders tells the story of his client, TailWind Voice and Data, an IT/telecom services company in Minneapolis. They turned over 60% of the company in two years once they focused on having the right people in the right seats. This created a team environment with highly accountable employees, a greatly improved culture, and the largest sales pipeline in company history. TailWind was on track to surpass $30 million in revenue.

As a Visionary, you choose who works *for* you. As a leadership team member, you choose who works *with* you. Only choose people that have your Core Values.

A joke that makes this point features a construction company that was hiring. They put a big "Help Wanted" sign out in front of one of their construction projects. A man saw the sign, smiled, and walked up to the foreman, who happened to be a pretty big guy.

When they made eye contact, the man said, "I want the job." The foreman looked him up and down and said, "We're not hiring."

The man was surprised and a little frustrated. He asked, "What? I see your sign out front. I want the job, so why won't you hire me?"

The foreman, getting irritated, said, "I'll be honest with you. Here at ABC Construction Company, one of our Core Values is 'Tough,' and you don't look so tough to me."

Now the man was getting angry. "Do you want to hear about tough? I used to be a lumberjack up in the Northwest, and one day I was cutting down a tree with a chainsaw. The chainsaw slipped and flew straight up in the air. When it came down, it chopped my left forearm off, and my arm fell to the ground. I picked my arm up, reattached it, and sewed it back on . . . myself. Is that tough enough for you, Mr. Foreman?"

The foreman said, "Holy cow! You *are* tough—you are hired!"

The man yelled, "Cool!" and stuck both arms out to give two thumbs up in celebration . . . only, his left thumb was pointing down. He had sewn his left arm on upside down.

Fortunately, "Smart" was not one of the construction company's Core Values and the man still got the job.

On the flip side, if you're a leadership team member or an employee, make sure you fit with your organization's Core Values. If you don't, it's time to move on. Other companies out there share your Core Values, and you will excel and love the people you're working with there.

LIFE IS TOO SHORT

Nowhere is it written that you are stuck with someone for life.

A lot of business partners don't get along because their Core Values don't align. In my experience, about half of my new clients that were partnerships didn't get along at the beginning of the EOS Process. (Forty percent of my clients are partnerships.) Of that half, about half were able to solve their differences, get on the same page, and enjoy working together again. The other half ended up parting ways.

When that tension exists between two partners, I start by saying, "Life is too short." I then ask them to imagine life 10 years from now if nothing changes. Then I ask, "Is it worth living this way?" With that clarity, half see a better life in the future without their business partner. The ones that part ways have always been very happy in their new endeavors.

In one initial presentation for a potential new client, I showed up and was instructed to meet one of the owners in their office alone. Then I had to go down the hall and do the exact same presentation for the other owner. How crazy is that? The two partners wouldn't talk to each other. They couldn't be in the same room together. Unfortunately, that gulf was too wide for EOS to help.

In a similar story, EOS Implementer Jason McCullough had an initial meeting with four leadership team members, two of whom were brothers. The meeting went extremely well, creating a lot of clarity, and the team decided to move forward with the EOS Process. Just before the first session, one of the brothers texted Jason to let him know that his brother would not be moving forward. He had decided that his brother did not hold the same values and they decided to part ways.

You must surround yourself with people you love working with.

Sometimes the entire leadership team has to be replaced. That's right: the Visionary realizes that every single person on their leadership team is the wrong person. This has happened with eight of my clients.

In one case, during the very first full-day session with one EOS client, I witnessed so much dysfunction, distrust, and infighting that the team barely survived the day. Several times, amid the nonstop shouting, people marched out of the session in anger. Yet the chaos created so much clarity for the Visionary that he knew exactly what he had to do. Within a year he replaced everyone with people he loved working with. Now he, the team, and the company are flourishing. Incidentally, two of the leadership team members that were removed are extremely happy at their new companies.

Overall, for a company that implements EOS, 80% of the time there is a change to the existing leadership team. Once your leadership team is made up of people you love working with, you go to the next level of growth together. Often this is one of the key barriers holding a company back from achieving its full potential.

This was the case with Nate Shea of SecureStrux, a $6 million company with 45 employees that provides cybersecurity services to the Department of Defense.

Once Nate gained clarity on the talent he needed on his leadership team, as well as the Core Values they must possess, he added two new members. The following year, he replaced his operations and accounting leaders and hired a new Integrator. Prior to these changes, their revenue had flatlined for three years; after making them, revenue rose 50%.

On a similar note, Tree Pros, a $5 million tree service company with over 50 employees, had hit a growth ceiling and struggled with profitability for years. Ironically, the leadership team had a highly skilled CFO in place. They valued his expertise and experience, but also struggled with his constant pessimism, gruff delivery style, and back-channel communications.

Once the team discovered their Core Values, they began to discuss them constantly and make them non-negotiable. Very soon, to the team's surprise, the CFO abruptly quit. They were devastated to lose his expertise, but quickly learned that the team had become more united. They promoted a junior leader with their Core Values who was passionate about the company and finance. Over the next year, they doubled net profits.

Reflecting back, the owner of Tree Pros realized how much putting experience in front of Core Values congruence was holding them back. Since then, the company has made a few tough moves in high-level seats for the good of the organization. Three years later, with a healthy leadership team, it continues to aggressively grow its top line while steadily adding to its bottom line.

EXPAND YOUR CIRCLE

To this point, we've discussed surrounding yourself with the people you love inside your company: your leadership team and all of your employees.

I now want to expand your thinking and ask you to consider extending this discipline to your clients, customers, and vendors. Do they have your Core Values? That's the ideal scenario. We EOS Implementers have the luxury of choosing our clients. We only work with the ones where we feel there is a really strong fit. On average, we each have about 20 clients at a time. We each have the joy of working with 20 amazing Visionaries, Integrators, and their leadership teams. Imagine how your life would be if all of *your* clients and vendors had your Core Values.

Ann and Sunny Sheu share the story of their family business, BT Furnishings, a $15 million furniture company with 90 employees. They used the People Analyzer on their vendors, suppliers, outsourced labor, and consultants. They eventually fired half of their partnerships when they realized there wasn't a Core Value alignment. Their Core Values are:

- Keep it real
- Better every day
- Create fun, Get sh!t done
- Passion for people

BT Furnishings stopped using vendors who could not "Keep it real" when it came to candid, open conversations. They fired suppliers who were not "Better every day" but were instead happy with the status quo. They got rid of consultants who did not "Create fun" and "Get sh!t done." These people were difficult to work with and didn't deliver on their promises. And most importantly, they terminated relationships with vendors who did not display a "Passion for people." BT Furnishings knew it wanted to work with vendors who were committed to taking care of their own employees, customers, and community. Sunny stated, "I remember thinking that certain partners weren't as effective or just weren't as fun to work with, but not really giving it much thought. After more intentionality and thought, we realized they didn't really share our Core Values as our partner. As we started raising the bar on the vendors we were working with, everything became more frictionless, and it just felt right. We definitely weigh this heavily when choosing new partners, and the People Analyzer is a strong, effective, easy-to-use tool to increase synergy and collaboration with partners, which in turn helps create a competitive advantage that is second to none."

Another great example of a company that expanded their Core Values circle is Payne & Payne Renovations & Design. They had long been a values-based organization. However, implementing EOS allowed them to synthesize and extend their Core Values standards to their trade labor partners. It became contagious.

As part of their process, they developed a rating system in working with their trade partners that centered around their Core Values. The results were extraordinary. Once-challenging trade partners became key relationships after they understood the standards, which allowed all to scale better together.

If you've never fired a client, do try it. Go ahead and People Analyze all of your clients, then fire the worst one. The one that drains your energy. It will be incredibly freeing. Please first make sure you are economically able to do so.

EXPAND YOUR CIRCLE EVEN FURTHER

Now, let's really expand your circle and hit close to home. Let's expand your thinking to your family, friends, and acquaintances. There's an old axiom that goes, "Show me your friends and I'll show you your future."

Consider being surrounded by people with your Core Values in your personal life. Imagine running everyone you know through the People Analyzer. You should realize that your personal Core Values may be different than your work

Core Values. That is not uncommon. If so, it's important that you discover your personal Core Values.

I love to help someone discover their personal Core Values. I can do it in about 15 minutes, thanks to powerful Core Values cards: a deck of cards where each card has a different Core Value. You can find them by doing a simple internet search using "Core Values cards." My favorites are by think2perform. I've used them with family members, friends, and anybody who wants to know their personal Core Values. You take them through a process of elimination, whittling the 52 cards down to five Core Values. It's an "aha!" moment for most people.

When Derek Pittak became an EOS Implementer, he hired an executive coach, Tim Carter, to help him develop professionally. He did not expect an in-depth look at his personal life, starting with discovering his personal Core Values. He stated, "It's ironic that as an EOS Implementer, I teach this to clients, but doing it for myself in a very similar fashion was fundamentally uneasy for me. However, when you are honest with yourself about who you are at your core and how you make decisions, it is undeniably freeing to make decisions or changes in your life with conviction. Overall, it really helped me think about who I want to surround myself with and what I want out of life."

His relationship with his wife improved tremendously. He made changes in some friendships—one that really hurt—which opened space for new friendships more aligned with his belief system. He said, "It is amazing what surrounding yourself with like-minded individuals does for your energy level, mood, and overall well-being."

EOS Implementer Peter Hammond shares this tough but impactful life decision about his family: "As one of twelve children, I went into adulthood thinking I owed each of my siblings equal time. After some life-changing events, I realized that I got energized by spending time with only five of them. I decided to unapologetically engage mainly with these five and treat the others as cousins."

Where are you on the spectrum of surrounding yourself with people you love? For some people, the answer to this question is scary, sometimes depressing. You'll see such a difference when spending time with people you enjoy compared to people you don't. People who are happy and surround themselves with people they love haven't done this by accident. They didn't get lucky. They are rigorous about removing "energy drainers" from their life, or staying away from them. You might have to make some tough decisions or have some tough conversations. Worst case, if you can't sever the relationship with someone who drains you, you might just have to reduce the time you spend with them.

Simply put, spending time with people you love being with, is living.

ACTION STEPS

Please write your answers to the following questions in your journal or on the Notes pages:

1. How close are you to being surrounded by people you love 100% of the time?
2. What would it look like to be at 100%?
3. Why aren't you there yet?
4. What would it take to get to 100%?
5. Who are the ones you love being with?
6. Who are the ones you don't?

Write down one thing that you will do in the next seven days to come closer to surrounding yourself with people you love. You may cancel an appointment you have scheduled next week with someone who drains you. Maybe discover your personal Core Values and People Analyze everyone in your life. Or you might make a change on your leadership team.

NOTES

_____
_____
_____
_____
_____
_____
_____
_____
_____
_____
_____
_____
_____
_____
_____
_____
_____
_____
_____
_____
_____
_____

Chapter 3

MAKING A HUGE DIFFERENCE

"The people who are crazy enough to think they
can change the world are the ones who do."
—Steve Jobs

Making a difference is all relative. You are the only judge
and jury. It depends on the impact you want to make,
the legacy you want to leave, the way you want to help.
Henry Ford said, "The whole secret of a successful life is to
find out what is one's destiny to do, and then do it."

How do you make a difference?

Take Five: Please take a few minutes right now and ponder this question. Write down in your journal everything
that comes to mind.

Your answer could be as simple as "Helping my clients
solve their problems," or as big as "Ending world hunger."
Jot down any of your thoughts.

Then rate yourself on a scale of 1–10. How close are
you to spending all of your time every day making a difference? A 10 means 100% of your working time spent
making an impact. That is the ultimate goal.

If you're a Visionary, you might want your company to
change the world. Or, if you're a sales manager, you might
want to help all of your salespeople earn six-figure incomes.
If you're an EOS Implementer, you might want to help the
employees of 100 client companies live their ideal lives. In
any of these cases, you're making an impact.

Truly making a difference is sometimes daunting or
uncomfortable to think about. Especially when you consider
another thing Steve Jobs said. He described making a difference as putting "a dent in the universe."

As an example, the Visionary of an e-commerce business realized that what he most loved to do was be a thought leader and to build a community around his company and clients. To accomplish that, he delegated the Integrator seat to one of his leadership team members and spent the next 18 months developing, creating, and writing. He packaged a talk, wrote an Amazon best seller, and launched a webinar series that became the gold standard for his industry association. He started spending the rest of his time talking with customers and arranging events where these business owners could net-work with each other and greatly increase their knowledge. As an ancillary benefit, his business benefited and became consis-tently profitable for the first time in its 20-year history.

As I mentioned, I had to delegate an entire company to free myself up to do what I love. I decided to sell EOS World-wide to focus on a new project and book I launched, called *Entrepreneurial Leap*, which can be found at e-leap.com. This 10-year project gives entrepreneurs-in-the-making a huge jump-start on becoming entrepreneurs and increasing their odds of success. My 10-year goal is to impact one million budding entrepreneurs and help them become what they were born to be.

You have an opportunity to build a company that will make a huge difference. Think of how you could impact all of your employees if you build a great company. Consider the impact you could have on all of your customers and clients. Imagine the families and communities whose lives you would improve. You may already be having this kind of an impact. If so, you can make it exponentially better.

THE EOS TOOL THAT MAKES THIS HAPPEN

This time we turn to the Vision/Traction Organizer (V/TO).

The V/TO has you and your leadership team decide on your Core Values, then gets you to agree on your company's Core Focus and set a 10-Year Target. It helps you crystallize your ideal target market and the unique message you will use to persuade it. With that nailed down, it guides you to create a specific plan for three years, one year, and the next ninety days. (If you are unfamiliar with the V/TO, you can download it at eoslife.com.)

Talk about impact! Once a leadership team is on the same page with their vision and plan, look out! You'll know exactly who you are, what you are, where you are going, and how you are going to get there. All the energy in your company will go in the same direction, and results will accelerate.

What impact will that make? Whatever you decide in the V/TO.

That's the beauty of knowing your vision. Once a team decides exactly what they want and commits to it, they get it. Let's start by looking at what happens when you decide what kind of an impact you want to make.

Josh and Christin Cherry, along with partners Cassie and Robby Marlow, are the four cofounders and leadership team members of Delta Life Fitness, a franchise based in Magnolia, Texas. Josh stated, "Growing a business is hard, and it's even harder with partners, multiple stakeholders, and family. It is hard to get everyone and all franchisees speaking the same language and working toward common goals."

They worked hard to get on the same page with a united vision for the company. They decided that the impact they want to have is creating positive communities of women. Over a three-year period, they grew revenue 100% per year and expanded from 12 to 75 franchises in nine different states. Recalling the process, Josh said, "It makes me incredibly happy knowing we get to do what we love, with people we love, and truly make an impact."

Another example is that of Mike Brewer, founder and Visionary of the Brewer Companies, a plumbing business in Arizona that was growing fast and having a harder and harder time finding good help. Realizing that this concern was an industry-wide issue, Mike set out to change the supply chain. He joined forces with other commercial and residential construction companies all over Arizona, raised money, and created a statewide campaign promoting the benefits of a career in the trades. They partnered with the community college system and helped kick off a new Construction Trades Institute to open additional paths into the construction industry. In addition, they created their own training academy called the Brewer Craftsman Academy, a training program that helped people to learn the plumbing trade while getting paid. They produced countless stories of young people coming to work for them and within a year earning over $50,000—well on their way to being able to buy their first home, making more money than they ever thought possible, and living a better quality of life.

Finally, consider the story of Chris Roth, who acquired National Technical Institute (NTI), a small, technical trade school in Las Vegas teaching students heating, ventilation, and cooling (HVAC). When Chris purchased the 14-year-old company, it was generating a mere $269,000 in annual revenue. It was operating with the equivalent of one full-time employee and graduated a total of 71 students in their best year.

While this was a bit unorthodox for such a small company, Chris chose to implement EOS in the organization on day one. Fast-forward less than three years, and over 1,000 students had graduated annually from NTI's Las Vegas, Phoenix, and online campuses. With a 95% job placement rate, these graduates leave with the confidence that they will find meaningful work and establish a career for life. Chris has achieved success at NTI by building a first-class leadership team and a relentless commitment to the company's Core Values. NTI currently employs 24 people and is on pace to exceed $5.8 million in revenue with a gross margin of 67%.

In terms of making a huge difference, Chris has a passion for teaching and knows firsthand that education is the key to success. The typical student who enrolls at NTI arrives earning less than $35,000 per year. The average graduate can easily earn over six figures with solid job-market growth projections, excellent job security, and high earning potential. The students graduating from NTI are Chris's best form of advertising.

Chris's five-year Core Target at NTI includes improving lives through education and infusing over 10,000 industry-relevant trade employees into the job market with a 95% or higher job placement rate. Now, that's making an impact.

Yet you don't have to run a company to make a difference. Say you are running a department. You might ask: How do I make a difference if I'm running operations? Or finance? Or sales?

Building a world-class department *does* make a difference. Consider how you could impact your employees by helping them to do what they love and live their ideal life. Think about how you'll impact their families. Imagine how you'll make the lives of your customers or clients better by solving their problems and meeting their needs.

Peter Hammond, an EOS Implementer, shares a great example of this from the time when he was the Integrator of a computer-server manufacturing company in California. He found out one of his employees in the shipping department was homeless. Other employees were complaining to HR about his personal hygiene, since he had nowhere to shower. Peter's plant manager took the homeless gentleman under his wing and, once he discovered his obsessive attention to detail, got him promoted to the quality department. Eventually, people who once complained about him nominated him for a Core Values award because his teamwork made everyone look good. He accepted the award to a standing ovation from 100 of his teammates. Needless to say, that plant manager made a huge difference in this man's life.

CREATE MORE LEADERS

If you're at a loss as to how to make an impact, here's a simple way that will last for generations. Simon Banks said, "You are not a leader until you have produced a leader—who can produce another leader."

Wow! Think about how profound that challenge is. You cannot consider yourself a true leader until you have mentored and produced a leader that can do the same for someone else.

The number-one way you can have an impact on this world is to create more leaders. If you are a leader, you're in a rare position. Only a small percentage of the population has your opportunity.

Think about the people in your organization and accept the challenge in Banks's quote. If you do, you will leave a legacy that will last for many lifetimes.

Thiru Thangarathinam is the Visionary at MST Solutions, a Salesforce solutions provider. Thiru is the gold standard for strong, compassionate, empathetic leadership. Within the company V/TO, Thiru plans for each member of his leadership team to be able to run their own company within the next 10 years. He devotes his time and company resources to developing individual growth plans for each member. In turn, each leader is expected to develop their own team in the same manner.

It's important to understand that this accomplishment might take the longest of all of the teachings in this book, which is probably why it is the most impactful. A rough guess is that it takes 15 years to accomplish this. Break down each step and you'll see why. By the time you mentor someone to become a great leader, that is at least 5 years from now. In turn, they will need 10 years to create a next-generation leader. That's because they have to accumulate enough knowledge to mentor someone for their own period of 5 years. That adds up to 15 years if everything goes right. I urge you to get started now.

ACTION STEPS

Please write the answers to the following questions in your journal or on the Notes pages:

1. How close are you to spending 100% of your time making the impact you want?
2. What would it look like to be at 100%?

3. Why aren't you there yet?
4. What would it take to get to 100%?
5. How do you want to make a huge difference in the world?

Write down one thing that you will do in the next seven days to come closer to making a huge difference. You might decide how you want to make an impact on the world. You might meet with your leadership team and do the same. Or you might pick one or two people who you want to help become leaders.

NOTES

Chapter 4

BEING COMPENSATED APPROPRIATELY

"Those who do more than they are paid for, will sooner
or later be willingly paid for more than they do."
—Napoleon Hill

L et me start by saying that appropriate compensation is all relative. You may want to earn $100,000, $1 million, maybe $10 million per year. It's all "appropriate." You have to decide for yourself. What do you feel is the right amount? For some, a $100,000 salary is plenty; for others, making $10 million a year is not enough. I have clients that make $500,000 a year and clients that make $15 million a year. The level is simply a choice you make, and it is in direct proportion to the value you create.

Do you feel you are being compensated appropriately? How are you adding value for people? Can you create more value?

> **Take Five:** Please take a few minutes right now and ponder these questions. Write down in your journal everything that comes to mind.
>
> Then rate yourself on a scale of 1–10. How close are you to being compensated appropriately? A 10 means that you are earning 100% of what you want. That is the ultimate goal.

Randy McDougal, an EOS Implementer, had an impactful life experience that helps him keep the proper perspective toward making money: "As a child, I remember my aunt and uncle were poor and lived in a tiny house. They had creativity and big dreams and ultimately pursued those dreams, became very successful, and made more money than they had imagined. At one point my aunt said to me, 'You know, the best thing about having a lot of money is to be able to stop worrying about making more money and get on with what is important in life.'" Randy went on to say, "I keep the quote with me to remind me that making more money is only valuable as it brings me more freedom to do the things that are truly important to me."

THE EOS TOOLS THAT MAKE THIS HAPPEN

The first EOS tool is one we've already discussed, Delegate and Elevate. Making more money goes hand in hand with spending all of your working time in the top left-hand quadrant: doing the things you love and are great at doing. That's because every time you elevate yourself, you provide more value to people. The more value you provide, the more you are worth.

For 30 years I've been delegating stuff off from my bottom two quadrants, and elevating to the top two quadrants. One of the results is that I now make 25 times more income. Every time I free myself up to focus more on adding value for my clients, my income goes up.

The two go together. If you're sitting there saying, "I'm not making enough money," you have to do something for others in order to earn it. Said another way, if you don't feel like you are making enough money, add more value.

Ask yourself the tough questions. Are you providing enough value to people? Are you solving their problems? As Zig Ziglar said, you can have everything in life you want—if you will just help other people get what they want.

At Turbosmart, a manufacturer of engine performance parts in Sydney, Australia, a factory worker on the production line heard that one of the company's priorities was to establish a social media plan for marketing. He approached the head of marketing and said he'd love to help out with the project, offering his time after work.

The marketing leader was not only grateful that this gentleman was willing to work for free after hours, but also soon saw his ability. Upon finishing the project successfully, the head of marketing offered the factory worker the opportunity to help with the next big marketing project, and again, the worker jumped at the chance.

Within six months, he was recruited into the marketing department full-time, and his salary was increased by 36%. By taking a chance to add more value, he elevated to doing what he loved and got paid substantially more.

On a similar note, a young man was working in the home center of a big box retailer. He had just graduated college with a degree in computer science but had not found a job in IT yet. He helped a customer who was so impressed that he gave him his business card and asked the young man to call him. The customer happened to own a software company. The young man called the number and got the job.

He started out as a junior developer, working on very simple tasks. Yet the level of detail and value he added helped the company grow new revenue streams they had not identified before. Over the course of five years, the junior developer elevated himself to being a lead programmer and leader/mentor of new talent. In that time, he increased his compensation from $40K to over $150K.

In addition to Delegate and Elevate, the other EOS tools that will increase people's income are . . . all of them! The growth that occurs by implementing the EOS Toolbox in an organization has now been proven tens of thousands of times.

If your company doubles in size, you're probably going to make more money—assuming you're the right person in the right seat, you continue to grow with the company, and keep increasing your value. Faster growth and an increased bottom line create a rising tide that floats all boats.

Here are some typical growth stories from EOS clients.

One leadership team set a very aggressive three-year revenue and profit goal in their first year of implementing EOS. The team fully committed to it and began following EOS to the letter. Not only did they hit the three-year revenue goal, they exceeded their profit goal by 43%, and they did it in two years—one year earlier than planned! The Visionary/owner decided to give everyone on the leadership team a bonus equal to their full-year salary to acknowledge the value they created.

In another case, a telecom company in New England grew from $40 million to $120 million in three years. They increased profit from 5% to over 10%—that's $2 million to $12 million. Everyone received substantial incentive pay.

In a humorous example, one client was stuck at the same revenue for three years before running on EOS. Nothing they tried worked. But by fully implementing EOS in their first year, they grew 35%. One of the leaders drove to the next session in a brand-new Chevy truck, rolled down the window, and yelled to his EOS Implementer, "This is all EOS's fault!" He hadn't been able to purchase a new vehicle in nine years.

And a pest-control company in Dallas cleaned house after discovering their Core Values and People Analyzing everyone in the company. They eliminated half of their field staff because they didn't fit the culture. After the house cleaning, they found they actually generated the same revenue with half of their former staff. That created a huge jump in profitability, and everyone made more money.

UNDERSTANDING VALUE

Let's say you are currently earning $50,000, and you decide you want to earn $100,000. How can you add more value to reach that level of compensation? You help more people get what they want by solving their problems. You can do this for customers and clients, and/or coworkers and employees.

Here's a simple value equation. If you flip burgers, that's worth about $12 an hour. If you do administrative work, that's worth about $25 an hour. If you're a vice president, your salary might translate to $50–$100 an hour. (In each of these cases, I'm using a 40-hour workweek to keep the math simple.) If you're an entrepreneur making $1 million a year, that translates to $500 an hour. And if you're a top motivational speaker, you might make $100,000 for a one-hour talk.

Let's look at a hypothetical $10 million commercial land-scape company. The people who cut the lawns might make $15 an hour. Their supervisors might make $25 an hour. The general manager might make $50 an hour, and the owner might make $500 an hour. Again, compensation is based on value.

If you cut the lawns and you want to make $500 an hour, you are not providing enough value to do so. The only way to make that much money is to become the owner. They are worth $500 an hour because they took a risk to start the business. They are responsible for the livelihoods of 100 people. They are juggling countless resources and orchestrating all of the moving parts of the business to generate a profit, and they run the risk of going out of business on any given day. If you want $500 an hour, you must do the same.

I learned economic leverage from one of my business partners, Ed Escobar. He taught me that I was crazy to cut my own lawn unless I got joy out of it. I could pay a company $25 to cut my lawn. At the time, I was making about $50 an hour and wanted to make more.

For starters, it was a "holy shit" moment when I realized every time I gave up an hour of work to cut my lawn, I was losing money. Second, I realized that by paying a company, I both freed myself up to make more money and increased my energy level because I hated cutting my lawn.

The real "aha!" was when I realized I could apply that thinking to everything I do. Starting with my personal life.

I applied this to any kind of maintenance around the house. And I didn't always have to *work* with my newfound time. I could also spend those freed-up hours with my wife, my kids, and my friends, or reading great personal development or business books.

That was only on the home front. I also applied this thinking to my work life. I stopped doing $25-an-hour work and delegated it to my assistant, outsourced it, or just stopped doing it altogether.

Tom Kosnik applied the same principle. He and his wife own a small business, Visus Group, which creates peer group roundtables for business owners. They were basically sole proprietors until EOS came along.

Very quickly, Tom realized that he spent way too much time on administrative tasks. He wasn't spending enough time selling, cultivating relationships, and networking. Tom loves bringing people together. He hired an admin for all administrative work, which really freed him up. Going a step further, he hired a fractional (part-time, outsourced) Integrator to run the day-to-day. Within a few months, Tom added another roundtable, and today he continues to be freed up to focus on scaling the company.

If you are an entrepreneur or leadership team member, adopt this rule of thumb: never do $25-an-hour work. As I shared earlier, EOS Implementers are taught that once they land their 10th client, they should hire a part-time assistant.

Focusing on session work with their clients generates a lot more money than the hourly rate they pay their assistant. It's basic economic leverage. Everybody wins. I've mentioned my five-to-one return when I invest in someone to delegate and elevate to. It's easy math. Delegating and paying someone to do $25-an-hour work generates $125 an hour in value. It's a great return, and it resolves the fear of whether or not I can afford it.

It's a winning philosophical formula: money always follows value. If you do something you are deeply passionate about, which provides tremendous value and helps enough people, you will earn as much as you want.

ACTION STEPS

Please write your answers to the following questions in your journal or on the Notes pages:

1. How close are you to earning 100% of what you want to earn?
2. What would it look like to be at 100%?
3. Why aren't you there yet?
4. What would it take to get to 100%?
5. What are the ways you could add more value?
6. What activities or responsibilities can you delegate to spend more time on providing people more value?

Write down one thing that you will do in the next seven days to get closer to being compensated appropriately. It might be calculating your current hourly rate. It might be setting an hourly rate goal. Or it might be hiring someone to cut your lawn.

NOTES

Chapter 5

WITH TIME FOR OTHER PASSIONS

"The difference between successful people and really successful people is that really successful people say no to almost everything."
—Warren Buffett

You are not balanced if you're working 100% of the time. You are not complete. As the saying goes, "All work and no play makes Jack a dull boy." You should work hard *and* play hard.

What are your passions outside of work?

> **Take Five:** Please take a few minutes right now and ponder this question. Write down everything that comes to mind.
>
> Then rate yourself on a scale of 1–10. How close are you to spending 100% of your personal life doing the things you really enjoy? A 10 means 100% of your personal time. That is the ultimate goal.

For me, I love to travel with my wife, family, and friends. I love reading. I love going to movies. I also love golfing, bike riding, going for walks, and hanging out with family and friends.

If you're too tired to do the things you love outside of work, you're out of balance. You're going backward. You're burning out.

You must make time to rejuvenate. To re-create (hence the word "recreation"). If you don't, your family and friends may get tired of workaholic you.

WORK/LIFE BALANCE— THE MISCONCEPTION

There's nothing wrong with working a lot of hours. Some people love working 70 hours a week. They enjoy that schedule, and their family and friends are supportive. This chapter is not about minimizing your hours. This is about *deciding* your magic number of hours. It may be 30 hours a week, or it may be 80 hours a week.

Matthew Kelly makes this point in his book *Off Balance: Getting Beyond the Work-Life Balance Myth to Personal and Professional Satisfaction*. He asked the leaders of dozens of the world's best companies if he could interview people in their departments who were known to have "work-life balance." What he discovered after interviewing these people was that they actually worked an average of nine hours *more* per week than their counterparts did. Matthew points out that highly motivated employees gain both personal and professional satisfaction from what they do. He states, "They work hard . . . they enjoy the people they work with; they feel respected by their boss; they feel their work is making a contribution to customers' lives; they find the challenge of their work matches their abilities; and they know why they go to work each day."

The point is, it is okay to love your work and to work a lot of hours. It's just a matter of choosing the number of hours that still gives you time in your personal life to recharge, have energy, and pursue passions.

The way to carve out time for other passions is by taking control of your time commitment to your work life. You must create a non-negotiable container of time that creates a personal life for you—a "work container."

THE EOS TOOL THAT MAKES THIS HAPPEN

We indirectly assist you in gaining free time by teaching something called EOS Time Management. It says, you only have so much working time in a week.

For example, for the last 20 years I have been a 55-hour-a-week guy. That's my magic number. That leaves me time to be a good family man, remain balanced, and have plenty of energy in all of my activities. I feel like I can make an impact and have time for other passions.

In addition, I work 40 weeks a year (and take 12 weeks off). So, my work container is 40 weeks a year and 55 hours in each of those weeks. Not a minute more. That is my 100%.

We're all different. One of my clients directs everyone in the company to work only 35 hours a week. They generate about a 40% profit and are ridiculously successful. That time container works for them. At another client company, they all work 80 hours a week. That works for them and they, too, are very successful.

All that matters is that you decide your 100%—your work container.

Only then can you take control of your life. Because if you don't, the job will always be an ever-expanding, negotiable, insatiable beast that eventually will devour you. Let's say you set your 100% at 50 hours a week, 48 weeks a year. You must live by that. You must protect that with your life! Literally!

Think of the container as your work capacity. If that capacity is exceeded for a long period, you will suffer terrible consequences. For some people it's burnout. Some have their spouses file for divorce. Some lose all of their friends. You may take on so much stress that you have an adverse health event, like high blood pressure, stroke, or heart attack. To avoid these outcomes, you must manage capacity.

If you think about your seat in the Accountability Chart, you can determine the time commitment needed to do your job well.

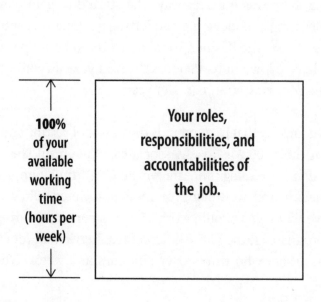

100%
of your available working time (hours per week)

Your roles, responsibilities, and accountabilities of the job.

If it takes 60 hours a week to fulfill your job responsibilities and you've decided your capacity is 50 hours, you are over your limit. It's time to delegate and elevate 10 hours of stuff in the bottom two quadrants.

Erin Figer is the Visionary for Core Consulting, a cloud alliance strategy and advisory consulting firm. As her business started to take off, she found herself still working too hard even after hiring the right people to support growing the business. She was working at least 70 hours per week, focusing on building her business. All she knew was to work harder. She was a single parent raising two daughters, and continued to sacrifice her own passions for the sake of her business and taking care of others.

As she implemented EOS in her business, she started to realize there was a better way. She started to gain comfort in delegating and elevating and letting go. One year into the EOS Process, she has her 100% down to 50 hours per week and plans to lower it to 45 hours the next year, all while growing the company 40% year over year.

A company that understands the power of setting and protecting their 100% is Roach Associates, a CPA firm. They have a passion for reimagining the typical CPA firm by improving the health and well-being of their associates. They don't believe that CPAs should work 75 hours per week during tax season. Instead, they have a Scorecard metric that identifies any associate who works over 50 hours in a week. When it happens, it becomes an issue that gets solved, because 50 hours is their 100%.

If your company is growing, the time it takes to accomplish your responsibilities will just keep growing. If your company grows 50%, a once manageable 50 hours a week will become 75 hours. Many leaders don't realize this has happened to them. They don't notice they have been slowly sinking in a quagmire. To protect your 100%, you have to get good at delegating and saying no.

THE POWER OF SAYING NO

"No" is my favorite word. I started this chapter with the Warren Buffett quote on the topic and am repeating it here because it might be the most important point in the entire book: "The difference between successful people and *really* successful people is that really successful people say no to almost everything." Being good at saying no frees you from the trap you have created for yourself.

I built EOS Worldwide with my partner, Don Tinney. Our deal was that I would give him 45 days a year as his Visionary. (The rest of my time was spent working with clients, writing books, and speaking.) I gave him 45 days a year for 12 years. As Don's Visionary, I had thousands of opportunities to do additional things to grow the company. I could have done 100 more talks each year, spent more hours with each EOS Implementer, or attended more brainstorming and strategizing meetings. But to what end? I had to set my limits and delegate all else, so that I had time for other passions. I had to say no at least a thousand times in those 12 years to protect my container.

THE EMPTY VESSEL

Here is the sad reality for many of you who finally get off the treadmill and decide to have a personal life: you realize you have no personal life. You have no friends, you have no hobbies, and your family doesn't really like you. And frankly, can you blame them? All you did was work, so now you are faced with a punch to the stomach.

You have one of two options.

Option one is denial. You can just go back to working 24/7 and pretend everything is okay.

Option two is changing your personal life. Take the time to do some soul-searching. Win back all of your family and friends that you have alienated all these years. If they won't take you back—which happens—find a new family and friends. I promise, you will survive.

Whether they take you back or not, you still have to decide your personal passions. There are so many to choose from. Life is so good. You could do nonprofit work, travel, hike, meditate, bike, run, walk, restore old cars, garden, hunt, play chess, build puzzles, fish, golf, exercise, manage your investments, run for local office, camp, go RV'ing, tailgate, watch sports, do pottery, ski, snowboard, play tennis, play pickleball, podcast, go on silent retreats, play board games, compete in an Ironman triathlon, make craft cocktails, paint, make music, sing in a choir, boat, cook, read, scuba dive, or learn to fly a plane.

If you already know your passions, gaining freedom from your undue workload and pursuing them will be like riding a bike. You'll start enjoying your passions immediately, and your energy and personal fulfillment will grow exponentially.

One Visionary who went from being out of balance to total freedom was Brad Martyn. He started from scratch, at the age of 40, Focus CFO, a business in the Midwest US that provides fractional CFO services to small businesses that don't need and can't afford a full-time CFO. With revenue in excess of $10 million per year, Focus CFO is one of the largest fractional CFO companies in their growing industry.

When he started the business, Brad was doing what he loved and was deeply passionate about the work. The early growth phase was exciting. He woke up energized every day.

Over the next several years, though, the business took off and started to expand. Brad found himself getting buried more and more in the day-to-day and working way too many hours. He was also spending a lot less time with the parts of the business that he loved—customers, new ideas, strategy. He was spending way more time *in* the business than *on* the business.

It got so bad at one point, someone once asked him how many hours he worked, and his response was, "All of them." Something had to change.

Shoot forward a few years later when one of his team members recommended they implement EOS. Brad was ready. EOS helped Brad get off the treadmill and back to what he loved. It helped him to build a strong leadership team, and he now has an incredibly talented and experienced Integrator in place. He now protects his work capacity, wakes up energized again, and chooses what he wants to do. He takes long vacations with his wife and family, and the only work things on his schedule each week, other than what he chooses to put there himself, are weekly meetings with his leadership team and Same Page Meetings with his Integrator, who calls what Brad does now pure R&D.

Another example is a client of EOS Implementer Bob Shenefelt who prefers to remain anonymous. He was a good friend of Bob's who finally reached out to him when he was at his wit's end. He was frustrated, burned out, and no longer wanted to be an entrepreneur. He was literally working 100 hours per week and sitting in 13 of 17 seats in his Accountability Chart.

Within a year, he hired great people aligned with his Core Values who filled all of those seats he was in. He was finally able to let go. He stays within his 100% and has grown the company fourfold. As a result, he was able to take his first two-week vacation with his wife. At a company event that

Bob attended, she gave him a big hug and said, "Thank you for getting my husband back."

THE ONE-MONTH-SABBATICAL CHALLENGE

For the last 20 years I've taken the month of August off. This is what I call my "one-month sabbatical." My goal is always to forget what I do for a living and hope that when I return, I still love what I do. Fortunately, I've always returned feeling that way.

A benefit I never anticipated was that this example would motivate our clients to take one-month sabbaticals themselves. One example is Tracy Call, owner and Visionary of Media Bridge Advertising, a 35-person company. Tracy did what she called the "Entrepreneur Stress Test." She wanted to test how she'd perform without her business and how her business would perform without her.

Tracy began preparing for her first sabbatical six months in advance. She described her preparation in three categories: operational, technological, and psychological. Operational entailed preparing employees and clients to operate without her for a month. Technological meant redirecting email, cutting off access to her email inbox, and removing apps from her phone that she didn't absolutely need. Psychological was mentally preparing to turn off her work life for 30 days and focus on her family.

Tracy's sabbatical was a huge success. Her team had a profitable month, landed some big new clients, and even made two new hires. But the larger benefits were on the personal front. Tracy realized how much of a barrier technology had become between her and her son. She also felt the sabbatical saved her marriage, one that she didn't realize needed saving.

The icing on the cake was Tracy's "aha!" to give her employees every Friday off during June, July, and August. That actually led to *increased* creativity and productivity.

Think of it as a dose of reality. Your business is not running well if you can't step away for a month and have everything still operate smoothly in your absence.

Now that many EOS clients have followed this example, I'd like to issue you the "one-month-sabbatical challenge." Take that time off, and once you return, please let the team at EOS Worldwide know by emailing them at eoslife.com so they can add you to the growing list of entrepreneurs that have "stress-tested" their business, as Tracy Call would say it.

THE PERSONAL AND FAMILY PLANS

As you can see, by knowing and protecting your 100%, you will create time for a personal life, and with a personal life you'll have time to pursue and enjoy other passions.

Now that you have this free time, you might consider downloading the Personal and/or Family V/TOs (also known as Personal and Family Plans) at eoslife.com. These tools are modeled after the V/TO and will be just as impactful for crystallizing a clear plan for your personal life and your family's lives.

ACTION STEPS

Please write your answers to the following questions in your journal or on the Notes pages:

1. How close are you to spending 100% of your personal life doing the things you are passionate about?
2. What would it look like to be at 100%?
3. Why aren't you there yet?
4. What would it take to get to 100%?
5. What is your work container?
6. What are your passions?

Write down one thing that you will do in the next seven days to spend more time pursuing your passions. Maybe it's deciding your 100%. You might pick a hobby or two. Maybe you can do the math to determine how much time it really takes to fully do your job well.

NOTES

Chapter 6

LIVING YOUR IDEAL LIFE

"Life is a journey, not a destination."
—origin unknown

Living The EOS Life is truly a journey. It's not a switch you turn on. It's not like "click," you're living The EOS Life. You have to make gradual progress every day toward living the life you were born to live. To start, you simply need to set a goal for yourself. Ten years from now, you will be living The EOS Life. If you accomplish it sooner, that's a bonus.

Every quarter, keep looking at the five points of The EOS Life. Keep mastering the EOS tools. Eventually, you're going to wake up one day and realize how far you've come. And here's the beauty: there's no end to how far you can go. Life can just keep getting better and better as you go deeper and deeper. Remember the model you drew at the beginning of this book, from page 10, where you illustrated the five circles around you: doing what you love, with people you love, making a huge difference, being compensated appropriately, with time for other passions. You just have to do a little bit of work on each of those five points every quarter. Improvement will be self-perpetuating.

EOS teaches that every leader must take Clarity Breaks. You set aside thinking time when you work on your business and yourself. Every great leader has their own formula for how they take their Clarity Break. For most it's a weekly event. Every quarter, during one of your Clarity Breaks, review your EOS Life journal notes, do a checkup on yourself, and ask, "What am I going to do next quarter to move closer to The EOS Life?" You might decide what to delegate this quarter. Or, you might decide to make one great people move each quarter. Or, you might add another personal passion to your list.

If you are disciplined and do the quarterly work, you might end up looking like the following people.

Chris Carlson grew up loving everything about the outdoors, especially racing snowmobiles. Working with his dad, he invented a simple but revolutionary snowmobile headlight cover that prevented snow from getting stuck in the light cavity. Soon other racers took notice, and asked Chris to make a headlight cover for their sleds—and the rest was history. Once Chris realized the potential demand, he offered to partner with snowmobile OEMs, and Sportech was born.

When he began implementing EOS, Sportech was doing $21 million in revenue with 65 employees and an incomplete leadership team. The company was growing, but lacked focus and accountability. He and his team quickly got crystal clear on the company's Core Focus and target market, got everyone on the same page with the company's vision and plan, and began making necessary changes to the leadership team.

Chris elevated himself 100% to the Visionary role. This freed him to spend nearly all of his time in his personal sweet spot: being a passionate leader, focusing on product research and development, developing people, and focusing on culture. He's also been able to invest time and energy in his various passions: spending time with his family; running the family race team, Carlson Moto; building a world-class racetrack and events venue; and spending time outdoors with friends, family, team members, and clients.

After 12 years, Chris and his team had grown the company to over $100 million in revenue and had dramatically improved profitability, so they decided to sell the company.

Not surprisingly, Chris capitalized on the opportunity created by the successful sale to continue pursuing his passions. He founded Envision Company, a family office dedicated to investing in and supporting family-owned and -operated companies that face the same challenges Sportech did in the early years—especially prior to implementing EOS. He remains committed to spending time with his family, his faith, and the outdoors—preferably while moving very fast.

Two EOS Implementers living The EOS Life are Alex Freytag and Tom Bouwer. They work with clients they love, are compensated appropriately, and are business partners who love working together.

Alex and Tom take what they call a Clarity Trip™ every year. This is a 1- to 2-week journey to beautiful, experiential places, where they can focus on their business and partnership at the 30,000-foot level—literally. They have traveled to places like Boulder, Colorado, Mt. Kilimanjaro in Tanzania, and Machu Picchu in Peru.

They uniquely combine all five points of The EOS Life in one trip. They are doing what they love, with people they love, focusing on how to make even more of an impact on the world. Their compensation enables them to go anywhere for their Clarity Trip, and it includes one of their passions, hiking.

Tom and Alex have been taking their Clarity Trips for a half dozen years, and on one trip they created the vision for the EOS Conference. Within three years their dream grew to a sold-out conference with over 1,000 attendees, and they have since sold the conference to EOS Worldwide.

Meanwhile, Karen Albright had always dreamed of owning her own business. Eventually, she opened a medical spa, BodyLase, in Raleigh, North Carolina. She absolutely loved the creative process of building a business from the ground up, and in the beginning, she worked countless hours. Her business continued to grow, and eventually she felt the business was running her, rather than her running the business. Roles and responsibilities were unclear, and since she didn't understand financials, she would just hope that at the end of the month there would be enough money to pay all of the bills and make payroll.

"Everything changed when I found EOS," Karen said. "The impact that EOS has had on my life and business has been nothing short of miraculous." Five years into implementing EOS, Karen loves her business again. She now has a strong leadership team in place. She reviews metrics every week, has a pulse on her business, and has plenty of money in the bank. She now goes to bed every night with a sense of peace that her company is thriving. The icing on the cake is that Karen now has time to devote to her next passion: mentoring women entrepreneurs to help them start and run their own businesses.

One last story of a person living their ideal life features Eric Lindsley, the Visionary at Knight Watch, Inc., a $23 million company with 100 employees that installs smart building controls and security in Michigan, across the United States, and in 24 other countries.

Eric starts by saying, "EOS has had the most significant impact on my life and business, more than any investment I have ever made."

After 22 years of moderate growth, Eric and his leadership team were burning out, working 60+ hours a week amid constant chaos, countless nighttime calls, and unlimited emergency meetings. Their families and health were paying the price. Something had to change.

Within two years of implementing EOS, they have more than doubled sales and quintupled their profits, and the leadership team is working substantially less, with less chaos. "The best part is our leadership team smiles more and we look forward to our meetings," stated Eric. "Our leadership team consistently accomplishes what we set out to do, and the stress has measurably diminished."

As for his personal life, Eric had this to say: "The best part of implementing EOS is my relationships with my wife, kids, extended family, and friends. I live more present now. When our youngest moved off to college, my wife and I took two months off and drove an RV across the country. I received two phone calls during that time. Both were to see if we were still alive and to let us know that we broke another sales record. The only reason we came back was for my quarterly meeting with my leadership team. Otherwise, we would have extended the trip another two months."

Again, the goal here is to move the needle on The EOS Life gauge. Keep striving for 100%.

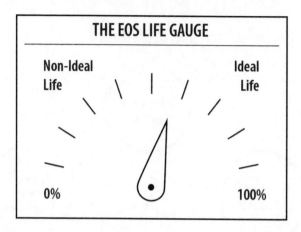

Once you clearly understand the five points of your ideal life, you will see opportunities to improve. Dan Sullivan says, "Our eyes only see, and our ears only hear, what our brain is looking for."

This is an iterative process and it is hard work. Greatness does not come easy. Jim Collins says, "Mediocrity stems from chronic inconsistency." You must consistently move the needle every quarter.

Let's return to the EOS Life Model at the beginning of this book, which you drew in your journal. Please turn back to that page in your journal and rate yourself on a scale of 1 to 10. Put your score in each circle. A 10 rating represents 100% achievement of that point. The objective is now to increase at least one of those numbers every quarter. If you do that consistently, you'll move the needle. You are striving to get to all 10's in each of the five points, which is utopian and borderline impossible. If you score all 8's, you are living The EOS Life.

The EOS Life Model

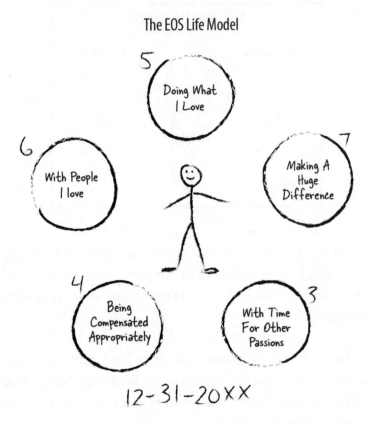

Now it's time to add the date (below the drawing) by which you will be living The EOS Life. Make a commitment to yourself. Earlier I mentioned 10 years, but it may not take you that long. You may have rated yourself all 7's and are living a pretty darn good life right now. You may decide you can do it in two years. Or you may have rated yourself all 2's and you have a long way to go. Ten years might not be enough.

Regardless, put a stake in the ground. Stop to calculate about how long it will take you to fully be living your ideal life. By committing to a date, you are starting the clock. You will need to be patient and treat this as a journey. Take it one step at a time and enjoy your progress all along the way.

The work you have to put in to live The EOS Life is hard. But it's harder to live an unfulfilled life. So, choose which type of hard work you want to do. The choice should be easy.

Before we conclude this EOS Life book and turn to the bonus mini-book, I'd like to share a wonderful added benefit. If you build an amazing life for yourself, you will become an example to the people around you. You will help them to live their ideal life.

Just think of the number of people that work for and/or with you, the number of people you come in contact with, the number of people who look up to you. It might be dozens, if not hundreds. How many would be inspired by you living your ideal life? Even if you just help two people live their ideal life, and those two people did the same, that would reach everyone on the planet in no time at all. And, oh, what a world it would be.

Imagine what your company would be like if everyone were living their ideal life. This will certainly take some work. But it has to start with you—you must be the example to start the chain reaction.

Also, remember that you can order The EOS Life Journal/Planner at eoslife.com. It is more than just a journal that is a great complement to this book. It is also a daily planner for your life and will greatly increase your productivity. And don't forget, you can download all of the tools and access resources at eoslife.com.

I wish you tremendous success on your journey.

Stay focused.

Now, on to the grand finale. Just when you thought it was over, it's about to get even better. This added bonus isn't actually a part of The EOS Life, but I was compelled to add it after I recently shared it for the first time with an audience of over 1,000 people. I was not expecting the reaction. I also was not expecting such a reaction from the 80+ test readers that read this manuscript.

They were so excited because it is a perfect complement to The EOS Life. It is a way to manage and maximize your energy. The following mini-book contains 10 disciplines that I have lived by for more than 20 years with great success. These disciplines, when combined with The EOS Life, will take your mindset, energy, clarity, and awareness to a whole other level.

I also decided to include it in the back of this book because I didn't think you should have to buy another book.

10 DISCIPLINES *for* MANAGING & MAXIMIZING YOUR ENERGY

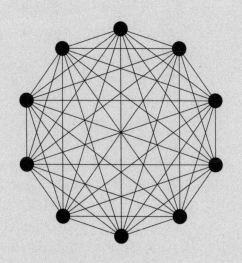

Gino Wickman

While EOS is a system for managing energy in an organization, which gets everyone focused in the same direction, we are now going to talk about managing *your* energy. I'm going to show you a system, made up of 10 disciplines, for doing so. Each one of them is fully customizable for you, because you are unique.

They are designed for the energy of an entrepreneurial leader. Since you have this entrepreneurial energy, we can cut through all the basics. We don't have to spend any time talking about leadership or management. We don't have to figure out how to motivate you. You're already motivated.

We also won't have to address exercising or eating right. Because I trust that you are already taking care of yourself.

With all of those givens, I'm going to take you to a different level because you are a racehorse. And you are ready to run. You merely need to harness your energy to run faster and win every race.

Each one of these disciplines is fast, simple, and powerful. They will help you expand, focus, and manage your energy.

At the end of each discipline, I am going to ask you to commit to taking action. So, please have your journal ready.

DISCIPLINE 1.
10-YEAR THINKING

This first discipline will literally transform your life. It transformed mine.

You are going to shift your mindset to thinking in 10-year time frames. If you're like most human beings, you are preoccupied with today, this week, this month, maybe this year at the most. This shortsightedness is limiting you.

When you shift to long-range thinking, time will suddenly slow down. A peace will come over you. You will start to make better decisions. You will become more consistent. You will be a better leader to your people. And the irony is that you will get to where you want to go faster.

I learned this discipline when I was 35 years old, and it altered my life. As has been said many different ways, "People overestimate what they can accomplish in a year and underestimate what they can accomplish in 10 years."

The reality is that you can accomplish anything in 10 years. As motivational speaker Les Brown once said, "All you need is a good decade."

Commit to the following three steps:

Step 1.   In your journal, write the exact date 10 years from now.

Step 2. Write the age you will be on that date.

Step 3. Take yourself there mentally, 10 years from now, at that age. Write down the number-one most important thing that you will want to have accomplished on that date. (You can write additional things that come to mind as well.)

You might have an income goal. It might be net worth. You might have a goal you want your company to accomplish. You might want to improve your physical health. There is no wrong answer. Yet, for this discipline to be productive, you must write down a long-range goal.

Next, think about everything you have going on right now. All of your goals, plans, activities, and what is on your current to-do list. Do they all align with that 10-year goal? If not, you have some course correcting to do.

For example, when I was creating EOS, I decided that I wanted to have 10,000 companies running on EOS within the next two decades. When I set that goal, only 50 were running on EOS. I had no idea how to get there. But we have spent the last two decades making 10-year decisions, and I'm happy to say that we achieved it, almost to the day.

During every 10-year cycle, you will experience ups and downs. If you are always focused on the here and now, you will lose sight of the big picture. You will get caught up in the current growth spurt, downturn, or crisis. By taking a 10-year view, you'll see, in the grand scheme of things, that a downturn is merely a blip on the radar.

My business mentor Sam Cupp taught me what he called the "10-year business cycle." He said, "Every 10 years you're going to have two great years, six good years, and two terrible years that can put you out of business." His advice has held up since he shared it with me over 30 years ago.

Whether a downturn is caused by a pandemic, a terrorist attack, a recession or depression, a war, or general business ups and downs, you know it's coming. You can count on one every 10 years for the rest of your life. The point is, don't be surprised by it. If you operate with a 10-year horizon, you will remain steadier and make better decisions.

The Great Recession of 2008–2009 was a blip in the grand scheme, although most of us with businesses didn't feel that way at the time. The same goes for 9/11 and the dot-com crash. I can go all the way back in history. They are blips.

The point is to be prepared. Knowing that it is going to come, you must have cash reserves. Always have six months of operating expenses in cash sitting in an account, both in your business and personal accounts, so you can endure six months of not bringing in any income.

Ten-year thinking is not so much about goal setting. You're reprograming your brain to think in a longer time frame. You'll make better decisions, and you will get to those goals faster.

Josh Holtzman experienced the amazing benefits of 10-year thinking when he owned and ran an IT services firm, American Data Company. When his company was generating $4 million in revenue, he set his eye on becoming a $40 million company in 10 years. Yet when he set this target, he and his leadership team had no idea how they were going to reach it. But once they committed, the answers came. Making 10-year decisions, the company joined forces with another player in their space. Unfortunately, they realized a few leadership team members weren't on board, so they replaced them with people who had greater experience and unflinching commitment. As you might imagine, they hit $40 million right at the 10-year mark.

Ten-year thinking will help you to burn less energy, because you'll stop worrying about the short-term small stuff. And it will increase your total energy because you'll have a long-range vision to motivate you.

When you go to bed at night, see, in vivid color, the most important 10-year goal in your mind. This will focus your thoughts and, if you believe in the law of attraction, increase the likelihood that you will achieve it.

DISCIPLINE 2.
TAKE TIME OFF

You can't go, go, go all the time. You have to turn your brain off. As Stephen Covey said, "You have to 'sharpen the saw.'"

You have to rejuvenate and recharge your batteries. You must work hard *and* play hard.

Chapter five taught how you should decide on and commit to a work time container that you must protect. On the opposite side, this discipline will ensure you are taking time off outside that container. Unplugging from work, turning your brain off, and recharging your batteries.

I take 150 days off per year (which includes most weekends). I've done it for over 20 years, and I'm convinced I'm further ahead because of it. I get more done, have more energy, and I'm more creative with better ideas.

When you unplug and then come back to the business, you view problems differently. You see them better. You see them clearer. As the old adage teaches us, "When I go slow, I go fast."

Entrepreneurs often push back by saying, "I can't take time off," "I don't like to take time off," or "That's not how I work." Some people just don't know how to turn it off. They're incapable of taking a break. They need to work. They feel like they're supposed to be working.

Please understand they have a disorder. They are workaholics. (Rule of thumb: any word with "-aholic" at the end is a disease and undesirable.) When you stop the grindstone, the healing begins. Just like during sleep, when you get the required one to two hours of "deep sleep"—the most restorative and rejuvenating stage—that's when your brain waves, heartbeat, and breathing slow down. Your blood pressure drops and your muscles relax. This stage of sleep improves memory and learning and produces growth hormones. Your energy is restored, your cells are regenerated, and your immune system is strengthened. All because you stopped and slept.

Imagine if you didn't sleep (or get enough deep sleep). It's the same as working all the time. You deprive yourself of the many benefits going on under the surface that you can't see until you take a break from work.

Todd Sommerfeld, the Visionary of Kreg Tool Company, a DIY-focused producer of woodworking tools in Ankeny, Iowa, has 250 employees and sells products through specialty and big box retailers. When Todd started the EOS Process, he was also the Integrator. He was trying to do it all, had his hands in everything, rarely took time off, and was burning out. And it was affecting his personal life. After the first year of implementing EOS, Todd hired an Integrator to free himself up, and by using the EOS tools, he started living The EOS Life. Todd finally started taking time off. When Todd's company graduated from the EOS Process, Todd's wife told their EOS Implementer, Alan Richardson, "EOS has given me my husband back."

Decide on the number of days off you will take per year. Commit to that figure in writing. Here's the simple math: if you're taking every weekend off, you're already taking 104 days off. Now add in your vacations and you'll have your number.

Please write your "days off" commitment in your journal right now.

DISCIPLINE 3.
KNOW THYSELF

This discipline helps you *be* yourself more than *know* yourself. But you can't be yourself until you first know thyself.

To start, you need to be comfortable and ready to let your freak flag fly, which simply means you being fully, unapologetically you. When we are fully ourselves, we appear quirky to others. The fact is that the world wants to judge us, and that squashes our light. The sooner you decide to be yourself 100% of the time, the sooner you'll have more energy. Because you won't have to fake it anymore. Being something you are not consumes a lot of energy.

As the saying goes, "Hell on earth would be meeting the person you could have been."

Knowing thyself is a matter of understanding your strengths, weaknesses, personality, and Modus Operandi (M.O.). There are many different approaches to knowing thyself. You can use profiling tools like DiSC, Myers-Briggs, Culture Index, or my favorite, Kolbe. I've taken at least 10 of them, and they've all had an impact on my clarity.

Another way to know yourself better is to get therapy. I've never met anyone that didn't need a little bit. I did in my twenties, and I'm grateful for what I learned.

Randy McDougal, a successful entrepreneur and EOS Implementer, shares his experience with therapy: "For me, therapy has given me the freedom to be vulnerable and curious about life and relational difficulties. It has made me comfortable being me, instead of feeling like I have to prove to those around me that I'm 'okay.'

"Through therapy, I've learned to separate my value as a person from what I do or do not do. I learned how in early life I developed 'compensations' to help me get through challenges. While most of my compensations are socially acceptable (working hard, keeping busy, making money), they are distractions and they can undermine me and those closest to me."

Randy also offers this advice: "Many people try one therapist and then give up. All therapists are not the same, and we each need to find the one who fits us and where we are in life right now."

Another way to know thyself is to get honest feedback from the people in your life. Ask them what they see as your strengths and weaknesses. Ask them what you do well and where you could improve.

This discipline of knowing thyself is much more robust than what you learned in chapter one, "Doing What You Love." In addition to operating in your personal sweet spot, which maximizes your skills and abilities, knowing thyself is fully being you 100% of the time. You fully express your personality, living by your M.O., acknowledging your weaknesses, and capitalizing on your strengths.

For example, learning and embracing that I was an introvert was incredibly freeing. I have never loved small talk and social gatherings, and I thought there was something wrong with me. Instead, I was just being the introvert I am, and knowing that was liberating.

The more you know yourself and live that way, the better you will function. You'll stop feeling apologetic for being who you are. You won't waste energy trying to be someone you think you're supposed to be. Have you ever felt you are one person at work, one person at home, one person out with your friends, and so on? You're trying to be all things to all people.

The textbook example of this happened when my wife threw me a surprise 30th birthday party. When I saw 100 people yell, "Surprise!" I was first excited, then struck by a sinking feeling of "Holy shit! Who am I going to be today?"

That's because I could see six different factions of my life in one room.

There were my employees and business partners. My family—mom, dad, brothers, and cousins. My wife's family. My high school friends. My entrepreneur friends, and friends from the neighborhood.

I realized I was literally a different person with each of these six groups of people.

With my employees I was "boss Gino." With my high school friends I was "crazy Gino." With my new friends I was "less-crazy Gino." And so on.

It was a wake-up call, and from that day on I was "authentic Gino."

Imagine the energy I was expending being who I felt I had to be with each individual group.

Now I am simply myself with everyone. I am hardworking, hard-playing, passionate, intense, beer-drinking, obsessive, introverted, gritty me. And being that way makes me feel a thousand pounds lighter.

Being someone you are not saps your energy.

So, who are you?

Please commit to one step you will take in the next week to move closer to knowing thyself. Maybe take Kolbe or one of the other profiling tools. Schedule a session with a therapist. Reach out to a friend, a family member, or a peer, and ask, "What are my three greatest strengths and my three greatest weaknesses?"

DISCIPLINE 4.
BE STILL

Whether you call it meditation, prayer, silence, or breathing, spend 10 to 30 minutes every day in silence. Being still will be transformative.

As an entrepreneurial leader, you go hard all day, every day. But at intervals, you must stop. Literally put on the brakes and just breathe.

I have been amazed at how closing my eyes and breathing shifts me out of my head and into my body. It centers me. It grounds me. It helps create absolute clarity on the project I'm working on, or the problem I'm trying to solve.

Every day that I wrote this book, my best ideas came when I was still every morning for 30 minutes.

Think of it this way. Imagine a glass jar full of water and a little bit of sand. Imagine shaking that jar. The water would be cloudy, murky, and unclear—like most of us when we go, go, go all day, every day. But if you let the glass jar sit for a few minutes, the sand settles and the water becomes clear, lucid, and calm. Just like what will happen to you, if you are still for a few minutes.

This discipline will increase and focus your energy. You will feel like you just drank a cup of coffee, but without the jitters or the caffeine crash 60 minutes later.

Rob Dube, co-owner of imageOne, a $15 million managed-print-solutions and software company with 50 employees, illustrates the power of this discipline with his own story. One day, he was on vacation with his family in northern Michigan just after selling their company (which they later bought back). It was a beautiful day, but he was inside his home working, feeling stressed, anxious, and out of control. He had recently read an article about mindfulness and meditation, so he decided to try it.

He chose a chair in one corner and sat in silence. The calm he achieved had such a profound impact on him that he made it a regular practice. This discipline led him to write a book titled do**nothing**, *the most rewarding leadership challenge you will ever take,* in which he teaches leaders the practice of being still. He also hosts the *Leading with Genuine Care* podcast and offers an annual silent retreat for those leaders who want to take this discipline to a deeper level.

Tomorrow morning, before you start your day, take 10 minutes. Sit quietly in a chair. Be still. Pause and breathe. See what happens. Do this for 30 days and see for yourself. It will have an incredible impact on your energy, your mood, and your relationships.

DISCIPLINE 5.
KNOW YOUR 100%

In chapter five, you saw that you should know the exact amount of time you will devote to your work if you want to maximize your energy. This is known as your "work container," which you must protect. What makes this discipline different is that it also works in the context of managing and maximizing your energy. You need to protect your energy. Deciding your perfect number of working hours will determine your peak energy. It's when literally one more hour of work would be less fun or start burning you out.

Think about your ideal time to wake up and what time you prefer to get home, along with how many days a week you want to work and how many weeks per year—your work M.O. This discipline, when followed religiously, maintains your high energy.

To illustrate, Meg Mayhugh runs her own consulting firm and has been on the leadership team as the head of HR and head of growth for several companies that run on EOS. She lives by this discipline and is extraordinary about helping people understand the concept of leveraging their time, both in her coaching and by her example. She is a single parent of three kids and works hard to be disciplined about both protecting her 100% and asking for and finding assistance. She delegates tasks unapologetically so that she can be a hockey coach, a volunteer board member at a local nonprofit, and a lifeguard. Juggling her tasks is not always easy, but she makes it look that way.

If you don't protect your container, where does work end? If work hours are negotiable, then you'll always operate above your 100% and you'll get burned out. You won't be the best version of yourself.

Write down your 100%, both the number of hours per week and the number of weeks per year.

DISCIPLINE 6.
SAY NO . . . OFTEN

With the first five disciplines in place, this discipline becomes easy. Your long-range plans are now clear, your time commitments are now clear, you know who you are, and you are taking time to be still every day. With this clarity, it becomes obvious what you should not be doing.

In *Essentialism*, a great book on the subject of simplifying your life, author Greg McKeown addresses the necessity of saying no. He states, "The very thought of saying no literally brings us physical discomfort. We feel guilty." He goes on to say, "Either we can say no and regret it for a few minutes or we can say yes and regret it for days, weeks, months, or even years."

McKeown also shares a great principle on how you should filter your decisions. He states, "If it isn't a hell yes, then it's a no."

You have to walk away from all the things that don't fit. The decision becomes as clear as someone asking you to eat a worm. You'd say no without hesitation. Every decision can be that easy. This applies to both your professional *and* your personal life.

You will reduce the guilt you feel by saying no because now your reason for saying no is so obvious. You will discontinue doing the things you shouldn't be doing. You'll no longer get sucked into doing things that drain your energy like they used to, when you would say yes.

Please write down one thing you've recently agreed to do when you should have said no. It might be an appointment that you scheduled, a project you committed to do, or an event that you planned. And then commit to saying no to at least one person this week.

DISCIPLINE 7.
DON'T DO $25-AN-HOUR WORK
(IF YOU WANT TO EARN SIX FIGURES)

I'm not knocking $25-an-hour work, and I'm not knocking people that make $25 an hour. We need people making $25, because that makes the economy work. If you are happy making $25 an hour, amen and hallelujah! But I'm assuming the reader of this book is either making six figures or more, or wants to make six figures or more. If my assumptions are correct, then you shouldn't be doing $25-an-hour work.

This discipline does not involve increasing your hourly rate as we discussed in chapter four (although you indirectly will). This shows how never doing $25-an-hour work will free up your energy.

You must eliminate all administrative tasks from your life. You shouldn't be checking emails, opening mail, managing your calendar, scheduling appointments, booking travel, or doing follow-up and follow-through work. Those things drain your energy. You must delegate them all.

Let's take checking your own email, for example. I dread checking and responding to email; it distracts me and saps my energy. As a result, I have not read or answered my daily email in over 15 years. My solution was simple: I hired an administrative assistant to do it. Every day I am free to do my craft and not get bogged down. Get an assistant to do your administrative tasks so you can spend all of your time in your personal sweet spot, which provides you with energy.

For example, the Visionary of a fast-growing international shipping company was still reviewing and approving every invoice before it went out. His executive assistant walked into his office late one night as he was poring over the invoices and asked, "Why are you doing that?"

The Visionary responded, "Because I'm the owner."

His assistant said, "It takes you two hours a day, it makes you upset, and honestly, you are not very good at it. Let me do it."

They put a process in place where she would approve anything under $50,000, and he would approve anything above. This freed up almost 10 hours a week for the Visionary to focus on growing the company.

In a similar story, a sales leader of a commercial furniture dealer shared with his leadership team that he hated doing contracts, but felt it was part of his job, so he just did it.

The head of finance offered, "We can review your contracts in my department so you can focus on sales."

This freed up hours of the sales leader's and the department's time to focus on building relationships and selling. These activities energized the sales team and grew the company.

Please write a list of all of the administrative tasks you are doing. You've just written a job description for your new assistant. Now, go hire one. You might only need someone for 10 hours a week or 30 hours a week, maybe full-time. But that person is out there waiting to take those burdens off you. Because that is what gives *them* energy.

DISCIPLINE 8.
PREPARE EVERY NIGHT

I've been practicing this discipline for 25 years. You should go to bed knowing exactly what you're going to do tomorrow. You have to hit the ground running when you wake up. This powerful discipline was taught to me by my mentor Sam Cupp.

Every night before I go to bed, I lay out my entire next day on a legal pad. I use a legal pad because I believe in the power of writing by hand. I time-block everything I need to do: the calls I need to make, the meetings I need to attend, the projects I need to finish. I list them all in chronological order so that my day is already charted.

If you do this, you will sleep better. You will wake up with ideas and be more creative. You'll wake up with answers to problems and projects you need to work on the next day. That's because your subconscious will be working on them during the night while you sleep.

If you are the kind of person who says, "I like to be spontaneous and let the day come at me when I wake up," or "I like to check my emails first and see what's in store for me today," or "I just react to the calls and problems that come at me in the morning," then you have lost control of your life. You're letting other people manage your energy.

EOS Implementer Tiffany Kruczek takes this discipline one step further. After preparing for the next day, she then spends some time with her eyes closed, visualizing the next day. She pictures herself doing everything confidently, on time and with the best possible outcomes. She feels it helps her day go smoother.

Please do this before you go to bed tonight: lay out the next day. You can do it on a legal pad or on a tablet, in your calendar or on any device you prefer.

Carry out this practice for an entire week, and decide for yourself if it works. I get such great feedback when people first try this discipline. You'll see right away how much it helps.

DISCIPLINE 9.
PUT EVERYTHING IN ONE PLACE

Let's take an idea from the last discipline one step further. I've been working from a legal pad for 30 years. My clients, friends, and peers lovingly laugh at my legal pad because it seems so archaic. It's always with me: when I walk into any meeting, when I'm on a call, when I'm driving. I live from a legal pad.

You can execute this discipline on any technology. It doesn't have to be a legal pad. Oddly, if I advocated using a tablet, many people would probably take me more seriously. But I recommend paper. As I've mentioned, I believe in the science behind the power of writing by hand. When you write things down that way, you retain them better.

Here's the typical day of an entrepreneurial leader. Let's assume you started working from the list you laid out the night before. As you work through the day, you have meetings and phone calls, you'll get ideas, you make commitments and promises to people, and you have to remember many work items. Normally, you put each of these to-do items somewhere, maybe on a sticky note, and set it aside. You might try to remember all of them in your head. You might tap them into your phone or text them to yourself. Yet, by the end of the day, you have compiled a mess of stuff you're supposed to do. And the truth of the matter is, you've probably forgotten some of it and you're about to let people down. Your brain can't keep track of all of that stuff.

At this point, I'm sure I don't have to tell you what that is doing to your energy. I'm guessing you lost a little energy just reading that paragraph.

In this discipline, you will put all of those items in one place. You first have to decide what that one place is. Your equivalent of a legal pad.

When I make somebody a promise, have an idea, need to remember something, or have to follow up on a task, I write it down on my ever-present legal pad. I capture it there so that at the end of the day, I can pull all of those commitments and ideas off the pad and put them on the list for the next day. Or, I might take care of some things right then and there at night while I'm preparing. I might compartmentalize others as to-dos in my calendar or time-block them as a project to work on two weeks from now.

The point is that you can organize all of those things at the end of the day when you have everything right in front of you. Also, by quickly writing all of the things that come at you throughout the day, you can concentrate on the task at hand and not get distracted.

Please try this tomorrow. Decide the one place you're going to put every single workday commitment, idea, and thought. Then capture everything that comes up throughout the day in that place. Try it for a week and see how it affects your productivity and energy.

DISCIPLINE 10.
BE HUMBLE

What does being humble have to do with managing your energy? Let me explain. First of all, I'm not talking about being weak. Humble people are powerful and strong. Pastor and author Rick Warren said, "Humility is not thinking less of yourself, it is thinking of yourself less."

Start by picturing a spectrum. On one end is "arrogant." On the other is "humble." I'm guessing you know both types of people.

Arrogant |————————————————| Humble

The definition of humble is, ironically, "your estimate of your own importance in comparison to others," and the definition of arrogant is "the way you view your level of importance in comparison to others." They are both saying the same thing.

What is your view of yourself? How do you view your level of importance in comparison to others? Simply put, humble people don't feel they are more important than anyone else. And arrogant people feel that they are.

To see how you stack up, draw the above spectrum, and then put a hash mark where you feel you are on it. If you want a more accurate depiction, ask someone close to you where they would put you on the spectrum.

Whether you are arrogant or humble, of course, you can be extremely successful. There are thousands of examples of both types of people. What I have discovered, however, is that the journey of life is better if you are humble. There is a universal law—the boomerang, karma, whatever you call it—that being humble in life attracts more humble people to you, which leads to more happiness, friends, and people that want to fight for you and be with you.

I am grateful for my father-in-law, Neil Pardun, for teaching me humility. When I was in my twenties, I was going down a path of arrogance. He altered the course of my life by his example.

He didn't even know he did it. He didn't pull me aside and say, "Hey, be more humble." He showed it through the power of his actions.

Neil was a wealthy man who made his money constructing industrial buildings, and who also owned a golf course. He was a tough guy, down to earth, authentic, and generous. He was always fully himself and didn't care what anyone thought. He treated everyone the same and always made you feel important. He was liked and respected by everyone.

I have two favorite stories about him. Once, while I was driving him home, he saw a set of ratty, dusty, used,

30-year-old golf clubs in someone's trash on garbage day. He yelled, "Stop the car!" He jumped out and garbage-picked the tattered old clubs because they could be used at his golf course. It was not beneath him to pick through someone's trash for something he thought was valuable.

The second story happened while he was working at the golf course. He would cut the greens every day while wearing his old jeans and a T-shirt. One day some young kids were horsing around on the course while he was on his mower. He rode over and asked them to stop. They asked, "Who do you think you are, old man?"

Neil said, "I'm the owner."

One of the kids said, "Yeah, right!"

You'd never guess he had money. I'm thankful every day that Neil was in my life.

In terms of energy management, when you are humble, you get more energy back from people than you put out. You also attract more people who mirror your attitude. Do you want to be surrounded by humble people or arrogant people?

Please list the five most important people in your life. Then reach out to each and ask them where they would place you on the arrogant–humble spectrum. This will help you determine how you are showing up in the world.

So, here they are, the 10 Disciplines for Managing and Maximizing Your Energy:

1. 10-Year Thinking
2. Take Time Off
3. Know Thyself
4. Be Still
5. Know Your 100%
6. Say No . . . Often
7. Don't Do $25-an-Hour Work
8. Prepare Every Night
9. Put Everything in One Place
10. Be Humble

Each discipline is easy to understand. Doing them is harder. Please don't underestimate them, as they will have a profound impact on your life.

If you do everything in this mini-book to maximize your energy and do everything in *The EOS Life*, you will be a force of nature. I urge you to review your journal notes every quarter during one of your Clarity Breaks and keep moving the needle. And when you are comfortable and ready, teach it to a few people.

Also, please go to the10disciplines.com for all things 10 Disciplines and the latest updates.

My wish for you is that you maximize your freedom, creativity, and the impact that you have on the world.

You deserve to live your ideal life and let your freak flag fly. I wish you tremendous success!

Stay focused.

Audiobook exclusive!

If you enjoyed this book,
get the audio for a **bonus
two-hour, in-depth interview**
with Gino Wickman.

Available where
audiobooks are sold.

ACKNOWLEDGMENTS

This book would not have been possible without the help and guidance of the following people. I cannot thank them enough for the impact they have had on my life. My heartfelt appreciation goes out to them.

Kathy, my strong and beautiful wife. I could not do what I do without your belief and support. I appreciate and love you with all of my heart.

Alexis, my incredibly wise daughter. You are as beautiful on the inside as you are on the outside. Your conscientiousness makes me so proud and you make me smile every day.

Gino, my quick-witted son. You are an engineer with an incredible personality. Thank you for always making me laugh so hard. I am so very proud of you.

Linda Wickman, my mom, for teaching me to be independent, for your amazing quiet strength, wisdom, and inspiration. You always make me feel so loved. I think about you every day and love you very much.

Floyd Wickman, my dad and my life mentor. This book would not exist without you. You are the entrepreneur's entrepreneur. You have taught me most of what I know about communicating with people, be it one or one thousand. You exemplify every principle in this book.

Neil Pardun, my father-in-law, for teaching me that it is possible to possess wealth and remain humble. You've helped me keep my feet on the ground all these years. You are a rare and special person. I am forever changed through your example. I miss you greatly.

Ed Escobar, my first business partner, for pushing hard and finally convincing my dad to let me into his company. Thanks for being so tough on me in my twenties. I now see how that transformed me. I am on this path because of your belief in me. Also, thanks for teaching me to never do $25-an-hour work.

Mike Pallin, who I truly believe is my guardian angel. You always place in front of me exactly what I need at that point in my life. You single-handedly altered the course of my life three separate times.

Karen Grooms, the world's greatest business manager. Thanks for holding all of the pieces together and protecting me from distractions for 25 years.

Curt Rager and Bob Shenefelt, for being an amazing sounding board and for constantly challenging me. Our annual trip to the mountains gives me tremendous clarity. You are lifers.

Don Tinney, the best business partner a guy could have. Thanks for fighting the good fight with me for 15 years. We built something great together. Also, thanks for branding The EOS Life and making it a "thing." If you hadn't, I would still be focusing on only the business results of EOS.

Sam Cupp, my business mentor, for teaching me most of what I know about business. I could not have pulled off that turnaround without your guidance. I hope I have done you proud with this book. I miss you greatly since your untimely passing.

The thought leaders who shaped my thinking in my twenties: Jim Rohn, Earl Nightingale, Les Brown, Napoleon Hill, Tony Robbins, Stephen Covey, and Brian Tracy.

Michael Gerber, it was your work that inspired me the earliest and the most. You are the original entrepreneur thought leader.

Dan Sullivan, for helping me discover my Unique Ability® and showing me how to build a life around it. You have made a great impact on my life. You are truly the coach of all coaches.

Verne Harnish, for being a pioneer and showing me that there is a place out there for my craft. Thank you for your passion and the impact you have had on the entrepreneurial world.

Jim Collins, for your amazing work, research, and inspiration. Your research on Core Values, core purpose, putting the right people in the right seats, and proving that "Level 5 Leaders" have a place in the world has simplified my work. You have truly changed the course of business history.

Pat Lencioni, for your amazing and unparalleled work. I've never met anyone with your combination of humility and talent. You are truly unique. Thank you for your words of wisdom on our drive to the airport. They changed my life.

Mr. Sarkisian, Mr. Long, and the late Larry LaFever, for looking at me and treating me as the person I would become when I was a teenager. You gave me confidence, and for that I am forever grateful.

Mike Paton and Kelly Knight, for succeeding Don and me in EOS Worldwide, and allowing us to pursue our next passions.

My support team, Lisa Pisano, Kristen Froehlich, and Amy Powell, for keeping everything running like a Swiss watch.

All of the people in the EOS Community, the EOS Worldwide leadership team, team members, and the EOS Implementers. You are truly putting a dent in the universe. Thanks for your commitment to the cause.

To all of my EOS clients, thanks for 20 amazing years. I still get excited before every session.

Story contributors, you are forever a part of this book. Thanks for bringing it to life: Karen Albright, Tom Bouwer, Mike Brewer, Tracy Call, Chris Carlson, Christin Cherry, Josh Cherry, Rob Dube, Erin Figer, Nathen Fox, Alex Freytag, Robby Hagelstein, Peter Hammond, Josh Holtzman, Tom Kosnik, Tiffany Kruczek, Nate Kukla, Eric Lindsley, Jeremy Macliver, Stewart Mahony, Cassie Marlow, Robby Marlow, Brad Martyn, Meg Mayhugh, Jason McCullough, Randy McDougal, Jason Nunemacher, David Payne, Derek Pittak, Steve Preda, Kevin Roach, Christopher Roth, Todd Sachse, Gregg Saunders, Nate Shea, Bob Shenefelt, Ann Sheu, Sunny Sheu, Todd Sommerfeld, Thiru Thangarathinam, and Trixie Whyte.

Test readers, thank you for your incredible insight. You are forever a part of this book and you truly helped make it great: James Ashcroft, Amber Baird, Matt Beecher, Tom Bouwer, Mike Brewer, Chris Carlson, Alexander Celie, Josh Cherry, Will Crist, Matt Curry, Ellyn Davidson, Daniel Davis, CJ Dube, Rob Dube, Susan Dyer, Michael Erath, Nathen Fox, Alex Freytag, Nancy Geenen, Gary Goerke, Ben Goetz, Joe Goudeseune, Haraya Del Rosario-Gust, Michael Halperin, Peter Hammond, Brandon Harris, Ryan Henry, Lisa Hofmann, Josh Holtzman, Catherine Juon, Jeffrey Kaftan, Kelly Knight, Pam Kosanke, Tom Kosnik, Tiffany Kruczek, Nate Kukla, Rob Laubscher, Eric Lindsley, Joe Mackey, Jeremy Macliver, Daniel Magill, Brad Martyn, Meg Mayhugh, Jason McCullough,

Randy McDougal, John McMahon, Drew McQuiston, Sandi Mitchell, Andrew Newsome, Mark O'Donnell, Scott Patchin, Mike Paton, Joseph Paulsen, David Payne, Philip Pfeifer, Derek Pittak, Steve Preda, Alan Richardson, Kevin Roach, Laurel Romanella, Bernie Ronnisch, Steven Ross, Todd Sachse, Gregg Saunders, Bob Shenefelt, Bruce Sheridan, Ann Sheu, Tyler Smith, Marisa Smith, Kris Snyder, Mark Stanley, Bill Stratton, Ian Switalski, Thiru Thangarathinam, Don Tinney, Mike Uckele, Bob Verdun, Carol Vitale, Jeff Wedren, Jon Weening, Trixie Whyte, Anthony Wood, Glenn Yeffeth, and Mitchell York.

Other contributors: my publisher, Glenn Yeffeth, and the team at BenBella Books; my editor, John Paine of John Paine Editorial Services; my illustrator, Drew Robinson of Spork Design Inc.; my fact checker, Veronica Maddocks.

And finally, to whatever higher power that was at work and called me to take on this project, I've never had more fun writing a book. Thanks for the calling.

ABOUT THE AUTHOR

 Gino Wickman has a passion for help-
ing people get what they want from
their businesses. He is the author of
the bestselling, award-winning book,
Traction, along with six other titles,
which together have sold almost 2 mil-
lion copies. He is the creator of EOS (the Entrepreneurial
Operating System) and the cofounder of EOS Worldwide,
one of the largest business coaching companies in the world.
There are over 100,000 companies using the EOS tools.
These tools help entrepreneurial leaders run a better business, get better control, have better life balance, and gain
more traction. Gino also delivers workshops and keynotes.